The Art of Making
Paste Papers

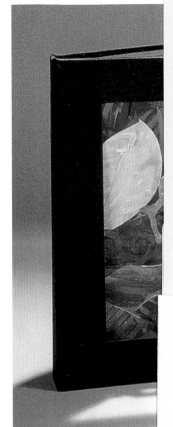

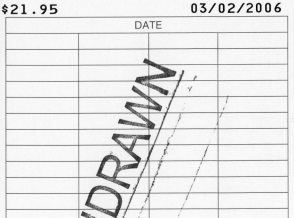

The Art of Making
Paste Papers

Diane Maurer-Mathison

WATSON-GUPTILL PUBLICATIONS

NEW YORK

FOR JOHN R. VOGEL,
MY FIRST FINGER-PAINTING PARTNER

First published in 2002 by
Watson-Guptill Publications
A division of VNU Business Media, Inc.
770 Broadway, New York, NY 10003
www.watsonguptill.com

Senior Editor: Joy Aquilino
Editor: Gabrielle Pecarsky
Designer: Areta Buk
Production Manager: Hector Campbell

Library of Congress Cataloging-in-Publication Data

Maurer-Mathison, Diane V., 1944-
    The art of making paste papers / Diane Maurer-Mathison.
        p. cm.
Includes bibliographical references and index.
    ISBN 0-8230-3933-1
    1. Paper work. 2. Decorative paper. 3. Paste papers. I. Title.
TT870 .M375 2002
745.54—dc21

                                        2001005537

Printed in Malaysia

First printing, 2002

2 3 4 5 6 7 8 9 / 08 07 06 05 04 03

ABOUT THE AUTHOR

Diane Maurer-Mathison is internationally recognized as an expert
in the art of decorating paper. Her work has been exhibited in
galleries and museums around the world and has been reproduced
by magazine and book publishers, stationery companies, and
manufacturers. Diane is the author of several books on paper art
published by Watson-Guptill, including *Paper Art* (1997), *The
Ultimate Marbling Handbook* (1998), and *Art of the Scrapbook*
(2000). She lives in Spring Mills, Pennsylvania.

ACKNOWLEDGMENTS

Sincere thanks to all the artists who shared their knowledge,
contributed projects, and allowed me to show their inspiring
artwork. Special thanks to Kimberly Byerly, Patti Quinn Hill, Paul
Maurer, Claire Maziarczyk, Virginia Passaglia, Mimi Schleicher,
Grace Taormina, and Kelsey Woodward.

NOTES ON THE ART

Front cover, clockwise from top left: *Send in the Clowns* (detail)
by Mary Howe; handbound books with paste-paper covers by
Beth Hale Beauchamp; lidded box by Kelsey Woodward; *Peacocks*
by Patti Quinn Hill. Back cover, clockwise from top left: *Folded
Boxes* by Mary Howe; a stamped dragonfly motif on a paste paper
by Diane Maurer-Mathison; picture mats by Myra Bendett; a basket-
weave design by Jeffery Mathison. Page 1: *For Flame Trees and
Bird Songs* by Anne-Claude Cotty. Page 2: *Peacocks* (detail) by
Patti Quinn Hill.

All line art provided by Jeffery Mathison.
All art not credited to a specific artist produced by the author.

Contents

Preface

The interest in making paste papers has grown dramatically in the past few years. Graphic artists are creating paste-paper designs to use in brochures and advertising art, book artists are using paste papers on covers, endpapers, and throughout their books, and calligraphers and painters are embracing paste-paper design and combining it with their painting and lettering work. Those interested in paper art and home decorating are also making paste papers to use in various projects, such as picture frames and treasure boxes. One reason for the popularity of paste papers is that the images are so varied and beautiful. Another is that paste-paper designs are so easy to make.

A centuries-old paper-decorating technique, paste-paper designs are made by brushing a coat of colored paste on a dampened sheet of paper and using various combs and tools to displace the paste and create graphic images. Its close relative, finger painting, is something most of us did as children. This is probably why, unlike marbling, batik, and many other surface design techniques, paste painting is so unintimidating. It is fun from the start. You can arm yourself with the most unconventional image-making tool—a spaghetti fork or a wadded up piece of newspaper, for instance—and produce a stunning paper with depth and dimension worthy of gracing the cover of a book of fine poetry.

Many paste-paper designers are reluctant to tell you what they used to create an image because they are afraid that the mundane and sometimes silly things they chose to work with will somehow diminish the value of the art they've created. My feeling has always been that the design created with a fifty-dollar paintbrush demands no more respect than the design created by flogging a pasted sheet with a handful of pasta. All things being equal, the spaghetti paper is more valuable because it has the added factor of the artist's ingenuity that went into the creation of the piece.

Another great thing about making paste papers is that you don't need any particular artistic talent to create successful designs. Yes, skilled artists can produce lovely paste-painted images by creating drawings or calligraphic designs in the paste, but you'll do just fine with simply a reasonably steady hand and some imagination. Even those people who consider themselves a little shaky when it comes to drawing a straight line can use tools to guide their hands, and they, in fact, may have an advantage when it comes to stamping a paper with a sponge or piece of clay to create an image.

In my paste-paper workshops, I've found over the years that many people love playing with the box of implements I bring, discovering on their own what kinds of interesting marks can be made by pulling, twisting, or stamping a tool into a pasted sheet of paper. Just as many people, however, require a more structured approach to making paste papers and want to know how to use the tools to make specific marks, or how to layer images to create intricate-looking designs. This book should satisfy both types of people. It provides patterning instructions for making specific designs and shows you what kinds of marks various tools can make.

This book also suggests how to use the paste medium in unusual ways to broaden the image-making possibilities of those who are already skilled artists and calligraphers. By viewing the work of a number of professional artists and paste-paper designers whose work is shown throughout this book and understanding their unique approaches to the medium, you'll see the limitless possibilities the paste-paper medium can afford you.

OPPOSITE, TOP: *From* Campo Santos, *an artist's book by Paul Maurer. Paste paper, rubber stamping, split pen work, pastel coloring.*

OPPOSITE, BOTTOM: *Paste-paper box by Kelsey Woodward. Photo by Jeff Baird.*

CHAPTER 1

Basic Equipment, Materials, and Techniques

Paste papers, close relatives of the finger-painted papers that so delighted us as youngsters, still captivate us as adults. The basic technique involves relaxing a sheet of paper by briefly wetting it in a tray of water, using a paintbrush to coat it with colored paste, and then drawing various implements through the paste to displace it and create patterns. Graining combs, hair picks, chopsticks, rubber stamps, carved brayers and potatoes, and lots of found objects can be used to make deceptively sophisticated designs.

OPPOSITE: *Using a rubber graining comb to create a scalloped design.*

Setting Up a Workspace

A large table is essential to setting up a workspace for paste-paper making. You need to have various tools, jars of color, paste containers, and brushes close by. You also need a place to store your paper, wet your paper, and dry completed designs. Drying lines can be set up in an adjacent room, if necessary. The paste cooking can easily be done in your kitchen or at a nearby hot plate hours before you begin creating designs.

If at all possible, set up the table on which you'll be working in such a way as to be able to walk around it. This will be an immense help when you begin creating patterned paste papers. Although you can work on a table that is a standard height, your back will be much happier of you elevate the table by placing its legs in 6-inch-long (15-cm-long)

Claire Maziarczyk's paste-paper studio.

sections of PVC plastic pipe. It is also helpful to have your lights positioned so that the glare of the wet paste doesn't reflect back into your eyes, making it hard to make precise lines when creating patterned papers.

Claire Maziarczyk, whose paste-paper studio is shown below, is one of America's leading paste-paper designers. Her large, open area—with two 4- × 8-foot (122- × 244-cm) paste-painting tables and a 42- × 50-inch (107- × 127-cm) wetting table—is essential for producing large 25- × 38-inch (64- × 97-cm) sheets. Claire keeps her custom tools close at hand on a nearby Peg-Board. A library of paste-paper notes is also kept nearby to refresh her memory about a pattern or to keep track of new discoveries.

Equipment and Materials

To begin your paste-paper adventures, you need the following equipment:

COOKING POT. A two-quart (2000 ml) saucepan is large enough for cooking up paste or mixing a methylcellulose recipe.

MEASURING CUP AND MEASURING SPOONS. You'll need these to measure the ingredients for making the paste.

TEASPOONS. You use these only for stirring paint into prepared paste, so they need be nothing fancier than old garage-sale items. Sturdy disposable plastic spoons can also be used.

SPONGES. These are used for wetting the paper, for making sponge prints in paste, and for cleaning up. Before using, squeeze out any soap residue that might have been left on sponges by the manufacturer.

GLOVES OR BARRIER HAND CREAM. Gloves will prevent your hands from becoming stained with color. Although most acrylics are nontoxic, you'll need gloves when working with colors containing cadmium pigments.

SMALL, PLASTIC WATER BUCKET. This gives you a place to dip the sponge when cleaning up and when sponging down the paper to be pasted.

LARGE, FINE-MESH STRAINER. Available from a housewares store, the finer the strainer the better.

BRUSHES. Several large, 2- to 4-inch (5- to 10-cm), high-quality house-painting brushes are needed—one for each color. Don't economize here, as cheap brushes lose their bristles (usually in the middle of a design). Foam brushes can be used with thinner pastes. A good brush is not too floppy or stiff, but has a nice, firm resiliency that will carry the paste across your paper well. My current favorite is a china bristle brush sold for use with oil paints.

TWEEZERS. For picking out any stray brush bristles or other debris that appears on your paper, tweezers are invaluable.

PASTE CONTAINERS. Plastic food-storage containers with tight-fitting lids are ideal for storing paste. They need to be wide enough and deep enough to accommodate the size of your paintbrush. Empty yogurt containers or wide-mouthed plastic cups can also be used. You can cover cups with plastic wrap when storing paste for a day or so.

WORK SURFACE. The ideal surface is a piece of Plexiglas that is at least three inches (8 cm) bigger all around than the paper you plan to pattern. Alternatives include a Formica or enamel tabletop or a flat work surface covered with plastic, pulled absolutely taut.

LARGE, SHALLOW TUB. A large, plastic storage box filled with a couple of inches of water is perfect for wetting your papers. You can also store your paste-paper equipment in the box between sessions.

PATTERNING TOOLS. Many household tools and found objects can be used to make paste papers. Plastic hair picks, forks, pastry wheels, buttons, rolling pins with decorative designs, and chopsticks are but a few of the many patterning tools you may already have on hand. Other great implements for making designs include potters' tools, plastic Spackle

Some of the non-combing tools used for patterning paste papers.

knives, and old credit cards. With assistance from an X-Acto knife, a utility knife, or some scissors, even corks, pieces of cardboard, and plastic milk cartons or plastic coffee can lids can be fashioned into paste-paper stamps and combs. Vary the tooth spacing on combs to give yourself lots of patterning options. Remember to coat any nonwaterproof materials like cardboard with an acrylic medium so they can be reused.

PAPER. Most nonabsorbent, medium- to heavy-weight papers are fine for making paste designs. The paper must be strong enough to withstand having tools drawn across it in a dampened state without shredding. Some of my favorite papers are Canson Mi-Teintes, Strathmore, and Mohawk Superfine papers, but many offset printing papers, cardstocks, and art papers also work fine. Heavy tag board and watercolor paper is used by many paste-paper artists. Charcoal paper can also be used as long as you are careful not to dig

into the rather soft surface that results from wetting it. Get a supply of colored as well as white papers. Black papers are especially attractive if they're covered with a gold or silver paste design.

PAINTS. Many coloring agents can be used to make paste papers. Tube gouache or a good brand of heavy-bodied acrylic paint, like Golden, Liquitex, or Flashe, gives excellent results. I don't recommend the fluid acrylics, as they tend to dilute the paste too much. Invest in the basic primary colors, black, and white, and add any other hues that appeal to you. Be sure to include some metallics and pearlescent paints.

PASTE. Rice flour, wheat flour, cake flour, cornstarch, and methylcellulose can all be used to make paste (or starch) papers. Glycerin (available at pharmacies) and liquid dish soap are also added to some paste formulas.

Techniques

MAKING PASTE

Many paste-paper artists swear by a favorite recipe. Others use multiple recipes, depending upon the type of image they are making or the tools they are using. Here are three recipes that I use. The flour paste is a bit stiffer and more granular in texture than the others, while the starch and methylcellulose recipes yield more smoothly patterned papers. A cake-flour recipe, contributed by calligrapher Nancy Culmone, is also included here. This recipe is a favorite of many calligraphers because it lends such a smooth writing surface.

Flour-Paste Recipe

4 tablespoons (60 g) rice flour
3 tablespoons (45 g) wheat flour
3 cups (750 ml) water
$1/2$ teaspoon (2.5 ml) glycerin
1 teaspoon (5 ml) liquid dish detergent

Blend the flours together in a saucepan with a little water. Then add the remaining water and cook the mixture over medium-high heat, stirring constantly, until it resembles a thin custard. Remove the paste from the heat and stir in the glycerin and detergent to keep the paste smooth and pliable. Let the paste completely cool and thicken before pushing it through a strainer to remove any lumps and then dividing it into bowls to be colored.

Cornstarch Recipe

$1/4$ cup (60 g) cornstarch
$1 3/4$ cups (450 ml) water

Mix cornstarch with $1/4$ cup (60 ml) water until well blended. Add 1 cup (250 ml) water and heat the mixture on medium-high heat, stirring until it resembles a thick custard. Remove from stove. Stir in $1/2$ cup (120 ml) water; the mixture will be quite runny at this

point. *Let it cool thoroughly, without disturbing it. It will take a couple of hours to rethicken. Once cooled, strain the mixture into a bowl.*

Nancy Culmone's Cake-Flour Recipe

6 cups (1500 ml) cold water
1 cup (250 g) cake flour (like Swansdown)

In a large pot, bring five cups (1250 ml) water to a rolling boil. In a separate container, mix the flour with the remaining cup (250 ml) of water until almost smooth. Slowly pour this flour and water mixture into the boiling water, stirring constantly. (The mixture will bubble up, so be sure to use a large pot.) Cook at a low-bubbling boil for ten minutes, stirring constantly. Remove from heat and immediately pour through a strainer into a bowl to remove any lumps. Cool before using.

Methylcellulose Recipe

Mix according to package directions, which may vary according to supplier. You want the paste to be about the consistency of toothpaste. Many people use Ross Art Paste (available in most art-supply stores) to make a methylcellulose paste. To do this, whisk 1 tablespoon (15 g) of the paste into 1 cup (250 ml) water (a tiny hand whisk from a housewares store works great). Let the mixture stand for about ten minutes before using.

The methylcellulose tends to give a more soft-edged image than I like, but many people use it because it is so easily made, it is less likely than other pastes to attract insects, and it lasts indefinitely when covered.

The first three pastes will begin to get moldy after two to three days, so make just enough for one paste-paper session at a time. (Unused paste that has remained covered can be refrigerated for up to a week before it starts to get

watery.) The number of sheets of paper you can create with each recipe will vary depending on how thickly you apply your paste. I usually find that four cups (1000 ml) of paste will allow me to produce about fifty 11- × 17-inch (28- × 43-cm) sheets of paste paper.

COLORING THE PASTE

Divide your paste among several cups, placing about ¹/₂ cup (125 ml) cooled, strained paste in each. Start by adding about two to three teaspoons (10 to 15 ml) of color to the paste, adding more, if necessary, until you reach the desired color. The quality of

your paint and its pigment will also determine how much you need to use. Be aware that the color on your dry paper will appear a bit lighter than the way it looks in the container. If you want to darken a color slightly, add just a tiny bit of black—though use it sparingly, as it can easily overpower another color. Metallic acrylics, like iridescent gold, silver, bronze, or copper, will add sparkle to your paste papers. Dry mica particles from a papermaking supply house or Pearlex pigments can be combined with your colored paste to lend metallic highlights and make your papers shimmer.

A basic color wheel showing the primary colors and the hues achieved by mixing them.

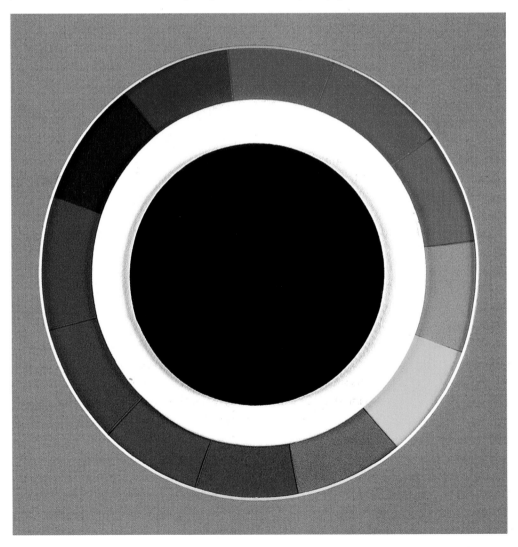

Basic Color Mixing

Although it is fine to work with a palette of colors straight from the jar or tube, there may come a day when your favorite indigo blue is all used up and nothing else will be quite right for the project you need to begin. It's helpful in such a situation to know a little about color mixing to give you the confidence to mix some black into your existing blue and come up with a color match. It's also sometimes more economical to start with some basic colors and intermix them to create additional colors to serve as your basic palette.

Unless you plan to work in a solid color, letting the marks you make in the paste be the focus of your creation (as many paste-paper artists do), choosing colors that complement each other will be an important part of your paste-paper designing. Your own color preferences can, of course, dominate, but, with some knowledge of how different colors are created and how colors interact with each other, you can more easily produce a successful multicolored paste-paper design. If you don't have experience mixing colors, spending a little time studying a color wheel will make your work easier.

By referring to the color wheel shown on the opposite page, you can see how mixing the primary colors—red, blue, and yellow—can yield a range of other colors or hues. The three secondary colors—purple, orange, and green—are made by mixing two primaries together (for example, red and yellow equals orange). The six tertiary colors are made by mixing a primary color with an adjacent secondary color (for example, blue and green equal blue green). Your color palette can be further extended by tinting these colors with white or shading with black to change their value and make them darker or lighter. In a composition, dark colors will appear to recede, while lighter ones advance.

Another factor to consider when choosing a color palette for your work is the *temperature* of your colors. Cool colors, like blue, green, and purple, appear to recede in a composition while warm ones, like red, orange, and yellow, leap forward.

Color Schemes

Four harmonious color schemes to consider for your paste papers are:

MONOCHROMATIC: Using tints and shades of a hue, such as light, medium, and dark green, creates a monochromatic color scheme.

ANALOGOUS: Create this type of color scheme by choosing hues adjacent to each other on the color wheel, such as blue, blue green, and green.

COMPLEMENTARY: By using one primary color and the secondary color opposite it on the color wheel, like blue and orange, complementary color compositions are formed.

TRIADIC: The combination of three colors that are spaced equidistantly on the color wheel, like red, blue, and yellow, create triadic compositions.

Other ideas for creating color schemes can be derived by looking around you at colors in nature to see how they complement each other. Your own flower garden or pictures in mail-order flower-gardening catalogs can inspire you. Look through art books, magazines, and home-furnishings catalogs to see what colors you prefer together. Wrapping paper, wallpaper, and fabric designs can also demonstrate pleasing color combinations.

Using a sponge to flatten and remove some of the moisture from the wet sheet.

PREPARING THE PAPER

To properly prepare a sheet of paper you should wet it in a tray of water. This will help to relax the core of the paper and make it easier to work with. You don't need to soak the paper; just drag the paper through the water, wetting both sides, and then let it drip for a moment before carrying it over to the Plexiglas and laying it flat. As you stroke the paper with a damp sponge, bear down to remove excess water, press out any air bubbles, and completely flatten the paper; if any wrinkles remain in the paper, your patterning will highlight them and make them even more noticeable. Wring out your sponge into a bucket of water as you work and pay special attention to the edges of your paper, where water can accumulate and run back onto your paste-covered sheet.

If you're working with small (11- × 17-inch [28- × 43-cm]) sheets of paper you can sometimes just dampen them on either side with a sponge. If you are using very thick papers—such as heavy watercolor papers or cardstock that won't wrinkle—and a rather liquid paste for an uncomplicated design,

you may also be able to get away with just dampening a sheet. But large, thin sheets of paper will wrinkle if not thoroughly dampened in a tray of water and will often dry out before you're through patterning them, so it's best to prepare the paper properly, as described above.

APPLYING THE PASTE

Solid Color Application

Fill a large, 2- to 4-inch (5- to 10-cm) paint-brush with paste and brush it evenly on your paper. Use horizontal strokes to cover the paper with a thin layer of paste and then go back over with vertical strokes to assure a good color application. If you find you have an excess of paste on your brush, wipe some of it back into your color container. In general, you'll want to use a minimum of paste, covering the paper well, but not applying it so thick as to leave thick ridges of paste as your tool passes through it. Papers with mountains of paste resembling a relief map might work as framed prints or as special papers for collage, but if you plan to do book-

binding or paper-art projects with your papers, there's a real danger of heavily applied paste cracking off the sheet when the paper is bent to cover a book or piece of mat board.

Multicolored Stripes

You can easily make multicolored striped sheets of paste papers. Work with several small brushes and use each to brush on a different colored paste. To preserve the stripes you'll have to brush in one direction only to avoid totally mixing the colors and making them muddy. Let the colored stripes overlap slightly to make subtle color blends. Different colored stripes running in a vertical, horizontal, or diagonal direction can form the basis for some great-looking papers.

Brushing a layer of paste on the flattened sheet.

Multicolored stripes of paste formed the basis for this paste-paper work by Jill Taylor.

Brushing through drops of paint to create a blue-green shaded paste paper.

Jill Taylor sponged on several different colored pastes to begin this highly textured paper.

Creating Randomly Striped and Shaded Papers

One of my favorite ways to create striped papers is to brush on a solid, rather light-colored paste and then shake on several colors of acrylic paint here and there on the pasted sheet. (Liquitex acrylics in small jars with dispensing caps are perfect for this.) After the colors are shaken on, use your original brush to make repeat vertical strokes up and down

the paper to draw the color drops into lines of color. The more you brush, the more the colors will mix into lovely shades and lines of color. If you continue brushing, you'll have a paper with subtle color shading. If you stop sooner, you can produce a paper with vibrant lines of color on a solid background.

Random Color Application

You can create multicolored papers by using small sponges or brushes to dab different colored pastes all over the damp sheet of paper. It's fun to have lots of cups of colored paste to work with when employing this technique. With this method of applying the paste you don't smooth out the paste by distributing it with a brush, you just apply a thin coat of paste and begin patterning it or let the textures and colors of the applied paste serve as the design.

CREATING THE FIRST PRINT

If you already have graining combs, calligraphy pens, potters' tools, or other craft items that might make interesting marks in the paste, assemble them for some new adventures. Otherwise, raid your junk drawer for chopsticks, swizzle sticks, corks, and other rubber, wood, or plastic flotsam and jetsam. You could cut up a credit card (this is much more fun than shopping) or even use one of those flat, plastic bread-bag closures to make marks in the paste. As long as your find doesn't have sharp edges that can tear the dampened paper, its possibilities as a paste-paper design tool should be explored.

Begin by trying all sorts of tools to see what kinds of marks they can make in the paste. Try producing repeat patterns, straight lines, curves, and squiggles to get your hands moving in a rhythmic motion. Begin your marks off the edge of the paper, on the Plexiglas border that surrounds it, rather than trying to line things up at the edge of your pasted sheet. If you don't like what you've created, brush on more paste and try again. The objective at first is to experiment. Although all marks you've made will show as "ghost images" below the final design, these can yield an interesting layered effect.

When you are happy with a design, peel the patterned paper off your Plexiglas and carry it by the top edge to a drying area. Let it drape over PVC pipe strung on a clothesline—the best drying apparatus. Don't let it dry on the Plexiglas, and beware of laying it flat on other boards. If any paste is clinging to the sides or the back of the sheet, it will adhere to the surface beneath it as it dries and rip when you attempt to remove it. (Unfortunately, I learned this one by experience—my all-time best sheet, of course.)

As soon as you've hung the sheet to dry, take a wet sponge and wipe off any paste marks that appear on your Plexiglas. You'll need an absolutely clean surface on which to begin the next sheet. Use your sponge to clean off any tools you've used at this point, too, to prevent your acrylic paint from drying on or in them.

Flattening the Sheet

If you hang your sheets over PVC, you'll minimize the crimp in the paper that results from its being hung over the drying line. If you hang the sheet over clothesline or on a plastic drying rack you will have to remove this wrinkle. Most paste papers curl a bit as they dry anyway, so you will probably need to press them under a couple of smooth boards or iron them on their unpainted sides to flatten them.

Cleaning Up

Before ending a paste-paper session, be sure that your Plexiglas and tools are absolutely clean and that brushes and sponges have been run under water and squeezed out to remove any paste or paint. Make sure your paste is tightly covered and your paint caps replaced so that your paint does not dry out.

A paste-paper landscape by Jill Taylor. Jill used credit cards and plastic tackle-box dividers as drawing tools to create this striking paste painting. 19 × 25 in. (48 × 64 cm).

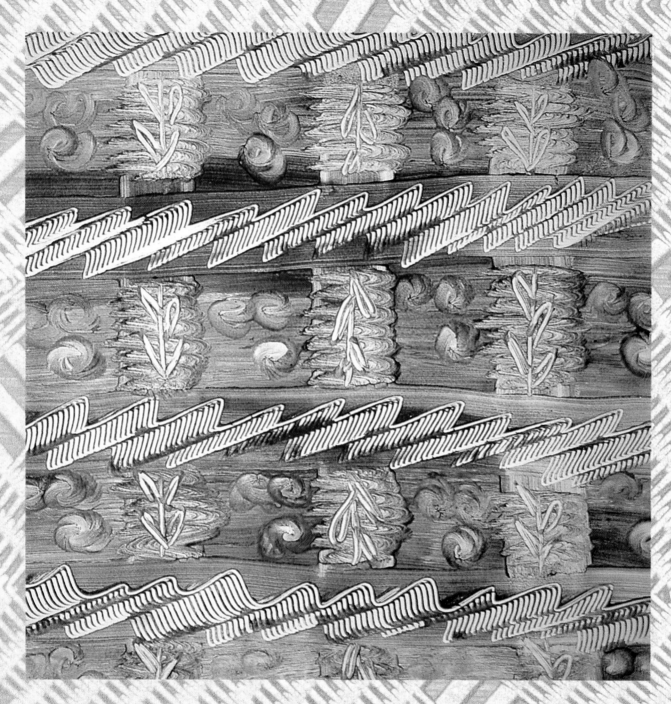

CHAPTER 2

Exploring Combed Designs

Combing is probably the most common form of patterning paste papers and one of the most versatile methods of creating designs. To make a combed pattern, you simply coat a sheet of paper with colored paste and draw your combing tools through it. As the comb moves, it pushes the paste aside and creates a corridor that allows the paper color to show through. Combed lines, curves, zigzags, and scallops can intersect, run parallel to, and overlap each other in myriad ways. You can work in various directions and come up with the most complex-looking papers that were anything but difficult to create. It's easy to get lost in the layers of overlapping patterns, however, so many designers take notes as they work so they can re-create their favorite pieces. In time, you will probably be able to untangle the patterns in the paste and determine which comb passes followed the previous ones.

OPPOSITE: *Swiss artist Virginia Passaglia created this colorful paper by drawing, combing, and creating thumb prints in the paste.*

Using Purchased Combs

Almost any type of comb will leave an interesting mark in your paste. Although most were designed for other uses, a variety of combs deserve a place in your paste-painting toolbox.

HAIR COMBS

Any tool with teeth that is not so sharp as to tear your paper has potential as a paste-paper combing tool. Hair combs, especially plastic Afro combs with widely spaced teeth, can be used to make various designs by displacing your colored paste as you draw the comb through it. If you apply pressure on the front of the comb, narrow lines will appear as you drag it down the length of the paper. If you apply more pressure, almost bending the teeth of the comb, the lines will be thicker as the wider part of the tooth makes contact with the paper.

RUBBER GRAINING COMBS

An inexpensive tool that makes combed patterns quite easy to create is the rubber graining comb. This comb is used to create faux graining and decorative finishes on furniture and walls. You can find rubber graining combs in paint and hardware stores. One type of graining comb is shaped like a triangle, with three 3-inch (8-cm) sides each having a different tooth spacing. There are smaller and larger varieties of this comb that make progressively wider parallel lines as you move it through your paste. A single-sided variety has graduated teeth that produce a series of thick and thin parallel lines as you use it. Both types of graining combs are small enough to hold in one hand to make multiple passes through the paste as you create combed patterns.

A wood-graining comb with a handle and a curved head is another type of tool worth purchasing for your paste-paper work. This comb was designed to produce the look of wood grain and knots in wood. It will give the same look to your papers if you rock it forward and back as you pull it toward you through the paste. The trick is to keep your hand in motion—you must be constantly rocking and pulling to produce the wood-grain design.

Another type of wall-decorating comb, used to make designs in paint, is about 12 inches (30 cm) wide and has a handle to use in manipulating it. This comb has rubber inserts that have narrow and wide tooth spacings. To use this comb you choose the size of the insert you wish to use, lock it in place with a metal bar, and proceed with

Some of the many tools that can be used to create combed paste-paper designs.

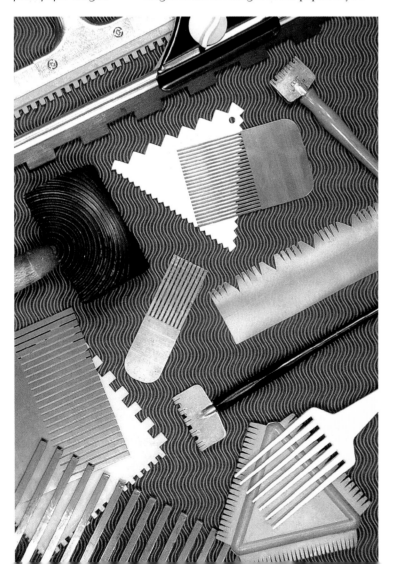

patterning. A single pass with this comb may be enough to lay down a pattern of lines as a basis for starting a design.

METAL GRAINING COMBS

Steel graining combs once used as faux finishing tools are still available today. Painters and woodworkers used them almost a century ago to give cheap pine doors and woodwork a grain pattern found in more expensive woods like chestnut and walnut. I found an antique set at a garage sale some fifteen years ago, but now have found the real thing reissued. The combs come twelve to a set in one, two, three, and four inches (2.5, 5, 8, and 10 cm) wide with teeth for fine, medium, and coarse graining patterns. Although they are made of metal, if used at a slight angle their teeth will not abrade your paper and they will yield some wonderful patterns in your paste.

Because the combs are made of thin metal, it's easy to bend some of the teeth out of the way to create your own even wider tooth spacing than the manufacturer provides and customize them for your own needs. Care must be taken to make sure that combs are always dried before being put away, however, to prevent rusting. Although they require extra attention, metal combs are worth the trouble.

MULTIPLE-LINE CALLIGRAPHY PENS AS COMBS

Multiple-line calligraphy pens also make great paste-paper combing devices. They range in size from $1/2$ inch to $1 1/2$ inches (1.3 cm to 4 cm) and are made of nonrusting brass. Because they are held in the hand like a pen, they give many people an immediate sense of control when used to pattern a paper. They can be found in art-supply and calligraphy shops.

A design made by pulling a rubber graining comb in a vertical direction.

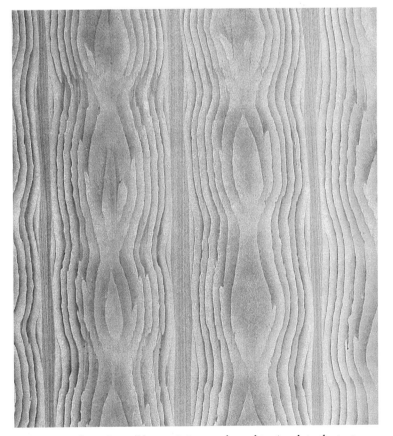

A design made with a rubber graining comb used to simulate the textures and knots in wood. The comb is continually rocked as it is pulled to create this design.

Cutting Your Own Combs

It's quite easy to make your own combs by cutting a strip of plastic from a milk carton or heavy plastic packaging material and using a pair of heavy scissors or a utility knife on a cutting mat to notch out your desired tooth pattern. If your plastic is sturdy yet thin enough, you can use pinking shears and decorative-edged scissors to make your comb.

Shower squeegees with a rubber edge can also be notched to produce combs of various widths and with different tooth patterns. Rubber door sweeps can be notched out to create wide combs that will pattern a paper in a single pass; get one with a slightly rigid rubber edge so it won't collapse as you draw it across your paper.

TIP

When working with combs, have a damp sponge ready to wipe off any paste clinging to your comb after each pass through your paste. That will prevent any excess paste from being redeposited on your paper and ruining your design.

TRICKS AND TOOLS TO GUIDE YOUR HAND

Many people worry that their combed designs look amateurish because their lines aren't totally parallel or straight. A little wobble here and there is acceptable and even charming in a handcrafted design. It sets it apart from a manufactured design. There are a few tricks and tools that you can try to diminish the shakiness you may encounter at first.

When lining up one row of lines parallel to the previous one, it will help to focus on the edge of the comb you're pulling instead of viewing the entire set of lines laid down. Angling the comb slightly toward you as you draw it through the paste will also make the work go smoother and put your hand in a more relaxed and steady position. If you really have trouble pulling a comb toward you in a semi-straight line, however, you may want to use an assist until you feel more comfortable with combing movements.

An artist's bridge, available through art-supply catalogs, is a sturdy Plexiglas shelf about 1 inch (2.5 cm) high and up to 24 inches (61 cm) long. Artists use it to support their hands so that they can add details to their paintings without smearing the wet parts. If you use a bridge that spans the width or length of your pasted sheet, you'll be able to create a straight line by running your comb along the edge of the bridge as you pull it toward you. It helps to get the longest bridge you can so that you can use it as a guide for diagonal lines, too, without worrying about accidentally placing the feet of the bridge in your wet paste as you reposition it.

You can create a makeshift version of a bridge by using a yardstick supported by a block of wood at either end. If you are really a perfectionist and want your lines to be not only parallel but equidistant from each other, you have my sympathies—I'm one, too. Here's my little secret: buy two adhesive-backed plastic tape measures and affix them in position on your worktable so you can measure out the distance between lines and position your bridge as you work.

A Patterning Guide for Combed Designs

It's great fun to just assemble a number of combs and start patterning pasted papers with reckless abandon, swooping in from the edge of the sheet, bisecting previous comb passes, and making short, choppy combed marks here and there. Everyone should begin paste-paper combed designs by just playing with their tools to warm up for more structured work. The patterning guide that follows will show you some of the straight, waved, scalloped, and freeform designs you can make with various combs. If you are working on a large sheet of paper and weren't able to set up your worktable so you can walk around it, rotate your Plexiglas as you work to comfortably reach all parts of the paste-covered paper.

STRAIGHT DESIGNS

By using various size combs and drawing them in horizontal, vertical, and diagonal directions, you can make elaborate patterned papers. The designs will look dramatically different depending upon the size of your comb's teeth and the distance between each pass of the comb. Patterns that look like gingham checks, architectural drawings, and contemporary abstract art can all be made depending upon how you use the combs.

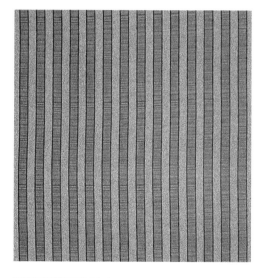

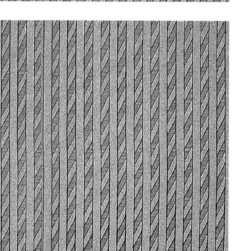

TOP LEFT: *A parallel set of vertical stripes made with a rubber graining comb.*

TOP RIGHT: *A diagonal right-to-left set of stripes made with a rubber comb with a slightly more narrow tooth spacing.*

BOTTOM LEFT: *This paste-paper design was created by combing diagonally over the vertical stripes.*

BOTTOM RIGHT: *An altered design results if you create the vertical stripes over the diagonal ones.*

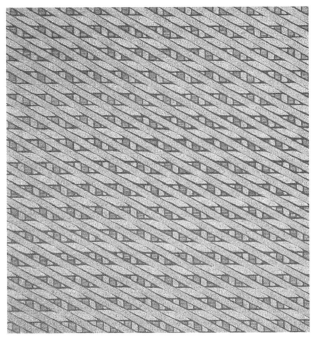

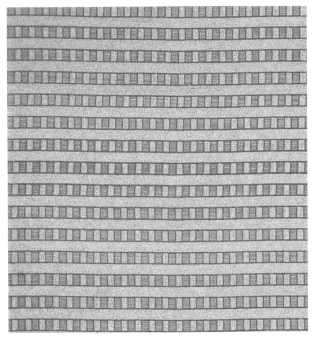

Horizontal combing over vertical combing creates this pattern.

Combing diagonally over the previous image creates this design.

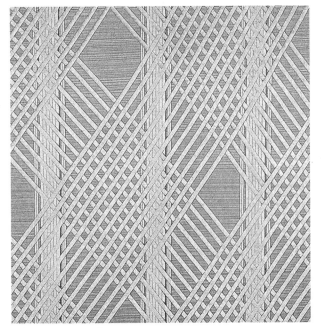

A calligraphy pen was used to create a set of vertical stripes to begin this paper. Diagonal stripes running from left to right were created over the vertical stripes with a metal graining comb. Diagonal stripes running from right to left (over the previous diagonals) completed the design.

A basket-weave design by Myrna Bendett, created by changing from a vertical to horizontal direction as she moved a metal graining comb across the wet paste.

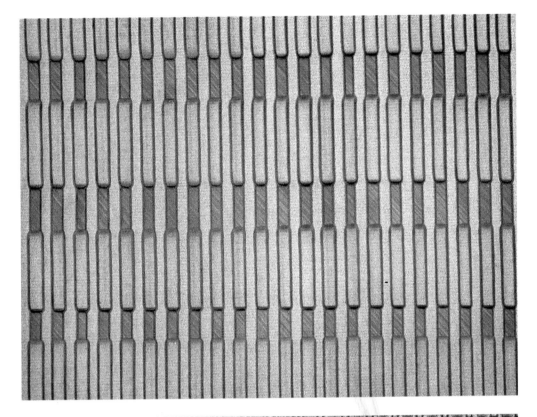

A combed paste-paper design by Mimi Schleicher. The paper can be made by creating a primary set of vertical stripes that run the length of the paper and then combing in between them for short distances throughout the sheet. You can also make this pattern by creating horizontal stripes with a very wide-toothed comb (see page 22) and then adding the vertical stripes.

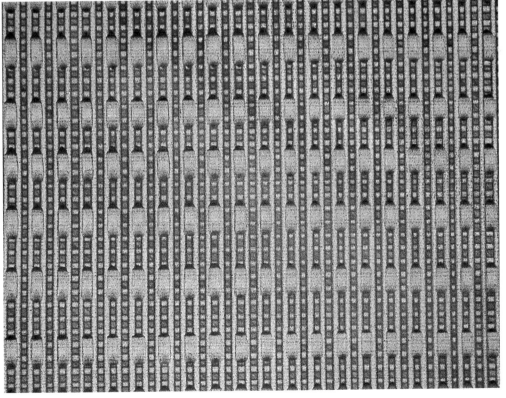

This very complicated-looking paper by Mimi Schleicher is actually not difficult to do, although it does require a steady hand! It consists of thin vertical stripes over horizontal ones (made with the same comb). A comb with a slightly wider tooth and tooth spacing is then used to comb between the vertical stripes, as shown, for a very short distance.

WAVED DESIGNS

Waved designs are perhaps the easiest type of combed design you can make. You can master gentle waves, figure eights, and narrow loops in no time. The movements are loose and fluid and feel very natural to most people as the combs dance across the page. Doing waved designs to light classical music is a great way to unwind and loosen up for tight patterning.

Waved diagonal stripes running from left to right create this paste-paper design.

Waved diagonal stripes running from right to left, made with the same rubber comb over the top design, create this patterned paper.

The break in the design created in this paper will show you the comb angles (diagonal over vertical) that resulted in this double-moiré pattern. The regularity of each set of waves is important to the creation of the moiré.

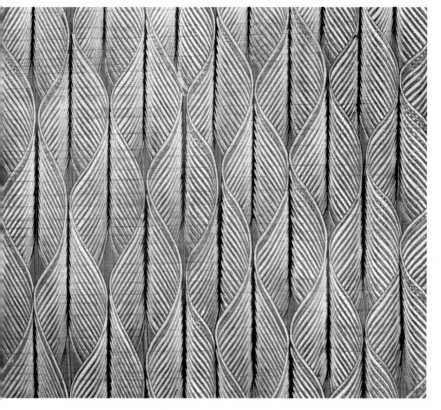

Dutch paste-paper artist Eva Van Breugel created this wonderful design with a small metal graining comb, a very steady hand, and much concentration. (The comb movement necessary to create this design becomes hypnotic.) Some people do this design with a comb in each hand, moving the combs simultaneously in and out to create the curves. Others use one comb and do one vertical curved line before moving on to the next, being careful to join interior curves. The trick to success is to hold the comb vertically, almost perpendicular to the paper, parallel to the paper's edge, and move it slightly from left to right as you draw it toward you.

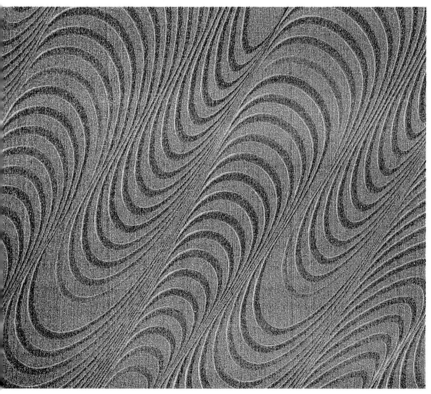

To create this design, hold a wide rubber comb on a diagonal and begin making a curved design. After moving about two inches (5 cm) across the paper to complete the top half of a curve, stop and slide the comb toward you as though slicing into the paste. Continuing to hold the comb at the same angle, begin a curve at the bottom of the sheet and then slice up again. Hold the same angle and continue across the sheet to create the design.

The step-by-step photos shown below and opposite feature Claire Maziarczyk creating one of her signature designs with a customized comb. Because she does production work, her waved design papers must match those she shows in a swatch book. She's devised a special jig to guide her comb for the first pass of each waved design used to create this paste paper—Gray-Blue V 10 R—assuring that this sheet will closely resemble other similarly created ones.

By placing a jig over some paste brushed on the tabletop, Claire uses a tool to scribe its pattern. (A series of combed stripes were made in red paste that was dried before the paper was rewetted, and blue, gold, and bronze stripes were brushed on.)

Using her comb, ingeniously created with hair picks, Claire follows the pattern of curves to begin her waved design.

Erasing the pattern created by the jig to begin a new patterning guide.

Using the new jig to create a waved pattern that will guide Claire as she creates a wider set of waved lines that intersect with the previous ones.

Combing through the paste using the guide lines created with the second jig.

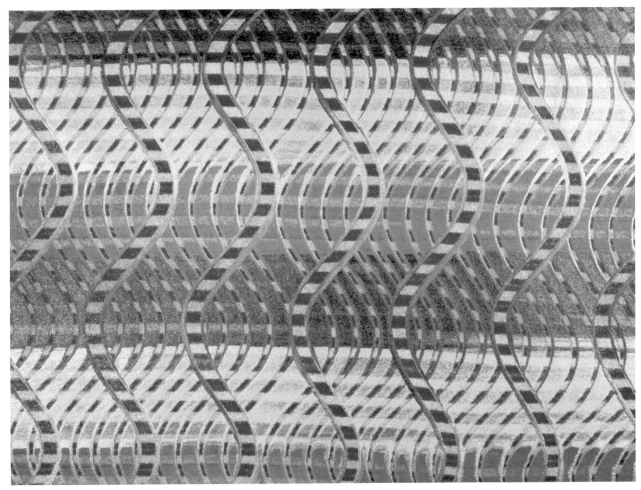

The finished paper, one of Claire's signature designs. Please respect Claire's copyright to the creation of this design.

SCALLOPED DESIGNS

Making scalloped designs is definitely my favorite way of using combs. You can work in various directions and achieve many different looks depending upon the width of your combs, the distance between their teeth, the tightness of your scallops, and the location of intersecting designs. Very complex and precise images can be made as you become accustomed to working with your tools and keeping your scallops a uniform size.

A three-inch (8-cm) metal graining comb, held parallel to the paper's left edge, was used to create this scallop design. The first row of scallops began at the bottom of the paper. The curves of the hill-shaped scallops are offset from row to row. The point created by the end of each comb pass is clearly visible, intersecting the center of a scallop from the previous row.

Diagonal rows of hill-shaped scallops begun at the lower right-hand corner of the paper intersect to form this design. A three-inch (8-cm) rubber graining comb was used to create the design.

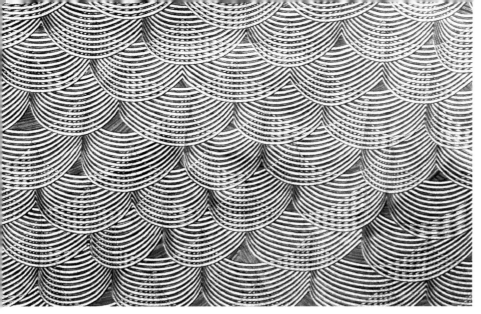

This scallop design, by Jeff Mathison, was made with a one-inch (2.5-cm) steel graining comb. The curve of each valley-shaped scallop hides the point created by the end of each previous comb pass.

The negative space between the rows of scallops is important to this design. Rows of left-to-right diagonal valley-shaped scallops are created with a three-inch (8-cm) rubber graining comb to begin this design. A space of approximately three inches (8 cm) is left between the rows. Then equally spaced rows of diagonal right-to-left-directed hill-shaped scallops are created over them.

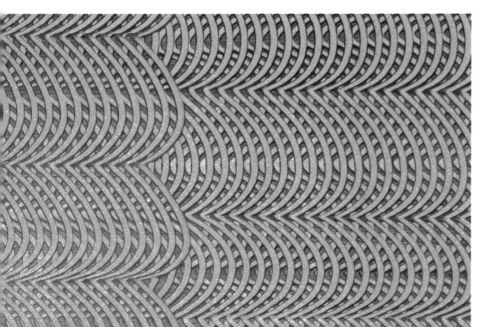

A ten-inch-wide (25-cm-wide) rubber comb with a handle was used to create overlapping hill-shaped scallops. The comb is held in a horizontal position at the top of the paper and moved right to left to create the horizontal scallop.

ZIGZAG DESIGNS

You need a fairly steady hand to master zigzag patterning, but a little practice will bring great rewards. Tiny herringbone patterned papers are quite beautiful, and contemporary zigzag designs have a vibrant energy to them that is unparalleled. By increasing the angle of the zigzag, many different designs can be made.

A double-zigzag design by Mimi Schleicher. A wide rubber-toothed comb was used to create a diagonal zigzag design in a single pass over the wet paste. The design was begun at the upper left-hand corner of the paper. Then a small one-inch-wide (2.5-cm-wide) metal comb was used to create additional rows of zigzags climbing from the bottom of the paper.

Jeff Mathison began this basket-weave design by holding a two-inch (5-cm) rubber comb on a diagonal and, without changing the angle, moving it in a zigzag across the paper. For the next row, he held the comb on an opposing diagonal and zigzagged it across the paper. By alternating the comb angle for each successive row and keeping the angle constant for each pass, a basket weave is created.

Myrna Bendett created this design of zigzags, which overlap in opposing directions, with a rubber-toothed comb that spanned the entire paper.

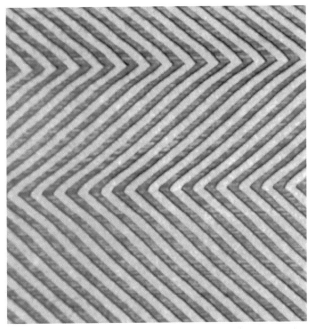

Jeff Mathison held a ten-inch-wide (25-cm-wide) rubber comb parallel to the top of the paper and moved it from right to left to create this preliminary zigzag design.

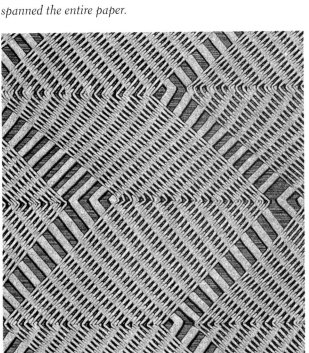

Jeff held a three-inch-wide (8-cm-wide) rubber comb parallel to the top of the paper and moved it left to right over the previous design to create this zigzag.

A zigzag design created by moving a rubber toothed comb held parallel to the paper's edge from left to right. The uneven sides of the zigzags and the fact that it was constructed over a series of vertical lines add to its complex look.

Combining Combed Designs

By combining various types of combed designs on the same sheet of paper, you can build a visually exciting multilayered image. The gentle curve of a waved line can become more pronounced when it is sandwiched between two straight ones. A row of straight lines can become a great background image to set off scalloped work created on top of it. A straight line that suddenly veers off to form a scallop can also produce a paper with lots of dimension. Another way to create dimension is to overlap the same pattern repeatedly and to create thick and thin lines by angling a tool as you move it through the paste.

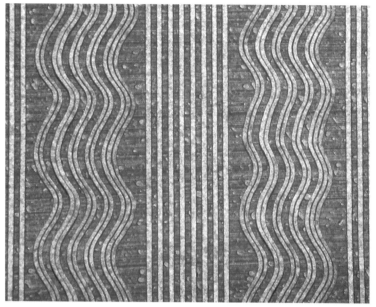

A multiple-line calligraphy pen and a metal graining comb were used to create this design of wavy and straight lines. The design below the combing was created with a textured roller.

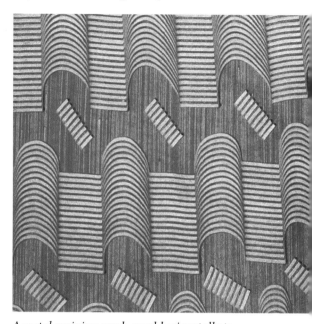

A metal graining comb, used horizontally to form straight and scalloped designs in the same pass, created a paper with lots of dimension.

Kimberly Byerly created ribbonlike thick and thin lines by angling and over-lapping various combs as she moved them through the paste.

Creating Repeat Accents in a Design

Large and small combs with narrowly or widely spaced teeth can be used to create an all-over patterned paper or to create repeat accents in a combed design. Try twisting, spiraling, and making choppy ¹/₂-inch-wide (1.3-cm-wide) marks with the combs instead of using them to create lines that span the whole paper. You can make fan shapes, corkscrew designs, chevrons, or tiny drawings in the paste with some practice.

RIGHT: *A one-inch (2.5-cm) metal graining comb was pulled upward and arched sharply off to the left or right to create this grasslike design.*

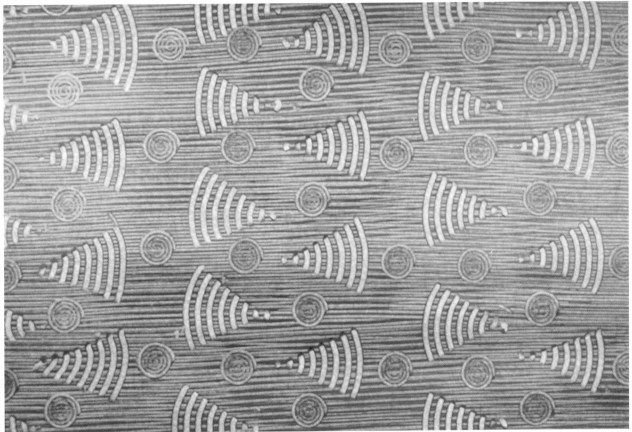

Metal and rubber graining combs and a stamping tool were used to create this design.

CHAPTER 3

Exploring Stamped and Textured Designs

Stamped and textured paste papers can be made in a variety of ways. Rubber stamps, carved potatoes, sponges, brushes, and crumpled newspaper can be used to create prints in paste. Found objects like buttons, bottle caps, and spools of thread can also be used as printing devices. When you see the results yielded by the odd things lurking in your junk drawer, you're likely to embark on a never-ending treasure hunt. Highly textured papers can also be made in several ways with spattering, pulled-paper techniques, and by using rubbing plates or stencils beneath a paper being coated with paste. Finger and palm prints can also yield great textured designs.

OPPOSITE: *A palm-print design was the initial image for this beautiful paper by Mimi Schleicher.*

Creating Stamped Designs

Purchased rubber stamps or stamps you've created yourself can be used to produce some delightful designs in a paste-coated sheet. You can either stamp directly in the unpatterned paste, create a background with a roller or brush, or use pulled-paper techniques to create a "canvas" for your stamped design. You'll need a good covering of paste, as it will be hard to push the paste away and make an impression in very thin paste applications. When stamping in the paste, the best impression is often made by wiggling the stamp ever so slightly as you press it in the paste. You may also want to wipe off the stamp with a damp sponge before moving it to another spot on your paper to continue the design.

Another way to use a rubber stamp is to coat the stamp with colored paste, paint, or ink just before stamping so as to add color when you stamp instead of removing it. Multicolored stamped designs can be created on top of a paste-covered sheet with this technique.

Testing and removing more of the background from a stamp created by Kimberly Byerly.

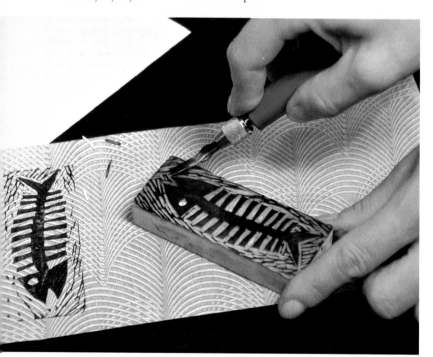

CUTTING YOUR OWN RUBBER STAMP

If you want to create your own stamp, you'll need the following:

ERASER. A Mars-Staedtler Plastic Grand Eraser, Pink Pearl, or other large eraser can be easily carved.

ERASER CARVING TOOLS. An X-Acto knife with #11 blades or a linoleum cutter with various sizes of V-blades make good carving tools.

PENCIL. A soft pencil will be needed for drawing designs on the eraser or tracing designs from other sources.

TRACING PAPER. For tracing designs from source material.

OPTIONAL EQUIPMENT. A ruler may come in handy. An alcohol-soaked cotton ball can be used to remove printed logos from erasers and transfer photocopied images from source material.

CHOOSING A DESIGN

The first step in carving your own stamp will be choosing and transferring a design to your eraser. Clip art, illustrations from magazines or books, or your own drawings can all become the basis for a rubber stamp design.

Simple designs without fine lines will be easiest to cut and will print best in the paste. The large fish-skeleton stamp created by Kim Byerly is a good example of the kind of image you might want to create. It is bold and graphic, without fussy lines that would be hard to cut and impossible to see in the paste.

TRANSFERRING THE DESIGN

Use alcohol and a cotton ball to remove any printed logos from the eraser, and cut the eraser to an appropriate size. Then use a pencil or permanent marker to draw directly on your eraser, bearing in mind that what you draw will print in reverse. If you trace a design from source material or create your drawing on tracing paper using a pencil, invert your tracing onto the eraser and rub the back of the image with a coin to transfer it to the eraser.

To create an enlarged or reduced image, simply photocopy it at a larger or smaller size before transferring it to the eraser. When you've resized the image, lay the photocopy facedown on the eraser and rub the back of the image with a cotton ball soaked in alcohol. Touch up the design with a pencil or pen if necessary.

CUTTING A SKETCHED DESIGN

Once you have well-defined lines to follow, it's time to begin cutting away the unwanted material around your design. Always make sure you cut away from your design so there's enough eraser remaining to support it for repeated stamping. Work slowly, using ink to stamp on paper, if necessary, as you cut, to make sure you're cutting deeply enough and removing the parts intended.

Push the V-shaped linoleum cutter away from you to remove parts of the eraser, remembering to keep the printing surface level. The X-Acto knife is especially useful for slicing out parts of a design and trimming away borders.

ALTERNATIVES TO CUTTING YOUR OWN STAMPS FROM SCRATCH

One way to create an original design without spending a lot of time cutting a stamp is to have your artwork laser cut and made into a rubber stamp. Check your yellow pages for a store that specializes in making rubber stamps. They can advise you how to locate a

laser-cutting establishment. Although laser-cut stamps are a bit expensive because the designs are usually sent off to be cut, lots of time is saved and the design is an original. Sometimes you can save money by ganging several images on one sheet of paper, having one piece of rubber laser cut with the images, and then cutting the rubber into separate stamps later.

Consider altering purchased stamps, too. A grid of small squares that leaves a great image in paste started out as a purchased stamp depicting a paper cutter. I just sliced off the paper-cutting arm and left the rest of the stamp intact. From another purchased stamp I amputated the postage-meter mark, leaving fine parallel wavy lines that would have been very time-consuming to cut. It, too, works well for paste paper.

Kim's fish stamp makes a great accent for her paste-paper flag book.

Design Principles and Repeat Patterns

When using a rubber stamp or another object to create an all-over repeat pattern (often called a "diaper pattern") in paste, remember that the unprinted areas between the images or marks you make will also define a shape and attract a viewer's eye. Many principles used in traditional print-making or rubber-stamp art that are critical to successful paste-paper design will become evident as you leave your marks in the paste.

Notice how the rhythm of your paste-paper designs varies as you stamp your images closer together or farther apart. A paste paper with a leaf stamped every four inches (10 cm) across the page would be incredibly boring to look at. The same stamp used to create images much closer together, with the images bouncing up and down, rotating, or going in different directions in alternating rows, would have much more energy. Don't worry about having the images line up exactly or displacing the paste in exactly the same way with your tool. The variation in the intensity and clarity of the image will add to your design.

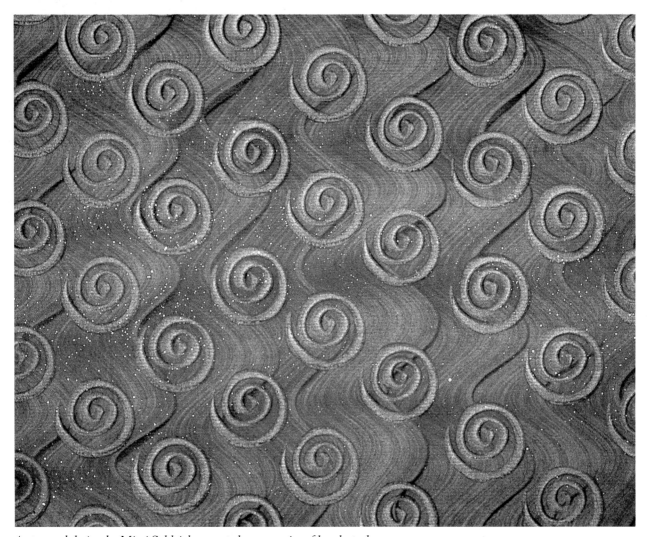

A stamped design by Mimi Schleicher created over a series of brush strokes.

Stamping with Found Objects

All sorts of found objects lurking in sewing baskets, toolboxes, and whatnot drawers are potential stamping devices. Plastic, rubber, cork, and wood will all leave impressions in the paste. Kelsey Woodward makes delightful papers with the imprints of clothespins, while Beth Beauchamp uses the throwaway plastic containers that house hardware store rubber bumpers to make designs in paste.

A trip through your local hardware, kitchen, or auto-supply store can yield lots of ideas for stamping devices. Watch for vinyl runners and floor mats with interesting designs to use as large printing devices. Remember that the surface of the mat must be even to print the whole design; if parts of it rise above the rest, only the elevated areas will print. Flea markets and garage sales are great places to scour for printing tools like old plastic game pieces, parts of puzzles, and old-fashioned kitchen tools that can be put to a new and more lofty use in your hands. Artist Peggy Skycraft, ever the innovator, recycles old rubber bathing caps to create some of her paste-paper designs.

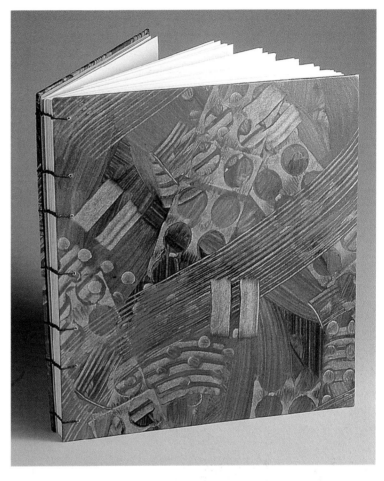

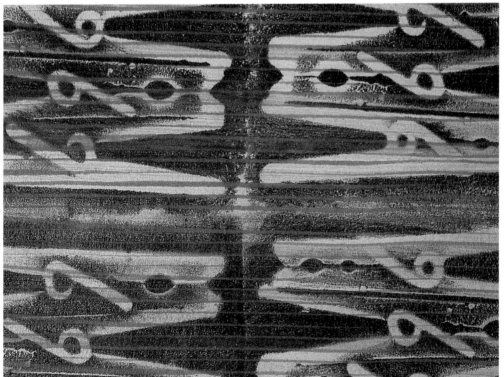

ABOVE: *Beth Hale Beauchamp often decorates papers to be used on her handmade books by recycling plastic packaging materials and using them to create stamped designs.*

LEFT: *Artist Kelsey Woodward sometimes uses clothespins to stamp designs in paste.*

Stamping with Printing Blocks

Wooden printing blocks used in India and Indonesia to print fabrics can be used to produce designs in paste. Antique stores and flea markets as well as import shops often have these for sale. Those with very detailed designs will be less satisfactory to use and must be cleaned immediately after use to avoid having paste and paint dry in their openings.

You can make your own printing blocks by gluing string or other objects on pieces of board, as long as the surface of the block remains even. Another option is to carve designs into soft block-printing materials, like Safety-Kut or traditional linoleum block. The same blades and carving gouges used to create your rubber stamp can be used on these materials. A woodburning tool can also be used to create designs in rubber or linoleum. For simple designs, outline a simple shape or shapes on the block and ink in all the areas you wish to print. Then remove all the extraneous areas.

More detailed designs can be made by removing interior parts of the design as well as borders. If your drawing skills are still evolving, you can trace designs from source material onto the printing block. Just remember that whatever you create on your printing block will show up as a reverse image in your paste. This is especially important to note if numbers or letters are part of your design.

Pieces of Buttercut, a soft, vinyl-like material with an adhesive backing, available from papermaking suppliers for blocking out parts of a mold, can be cut with scissors and adhered to a piece of wood to use as a printing block. Unmounted linoleum can also be cut and glued (with waterproof glue) to a block of wood to use as a printing device. Even self-adhesive corn and callous protectors, found in drugstores, can be affixed to woodblocks and used as printing devices.

Drugstores can also yield interesting printing devices. The foot-ailment department can offer great stamping pads.

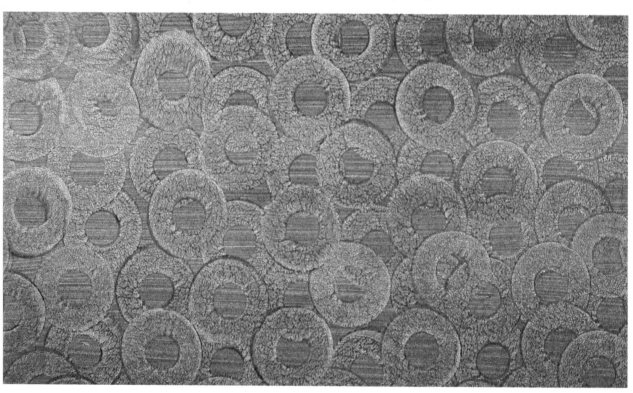

Additional Materials for Stamping

Materials like clay, paper, and plastic wrap can be compressed to form misshapen blobs and crumpled balls that look like anything but stamping devices. But just wait until you see the beautiful results you can achieve with these tools.

STAMPING WITH PIECES OF CLAY

Modeling clay, designed to stay soft, makes a great stamping tool. (I purchased some on a whim just to see if it would work. What fun! This may even lure me away from my scallop designs.) Just soften the material in your hands and make round or abstract shapes, leaving enough of a "handle" to let you stamp an entire sheet of paper. Gouge out parts of the clay with your fingernail to create an opening in a design.

STAMPING WITH NEWSPAPER, WAXED PAPER, AND PLASTIC WRAP

Beautiful all-over patterns can be made in paste by repeatedly stamping them with crumpled newspaper, waxed paper, or plastic wrap. A small, tightly crumpled piece of paper can produce a series of rosettes, while a larger wad of paper will cover more area and quickly give your entire paper a subtle, fractured look. Because your crumpled paper makes a pattern by removing the paste it strikes, on large sheets of paper you may have to turn the stamp to find a dry area to work with, or have several crumpled bundles at the fore to continue a pattern when your stamping device gets soggy.

As with rubber stamps, you can first coat your crumpled paper with paste and use it to apply various colored pastes over your previously pasted-up sheet. Although the impression left by the edges of the crumpled paper won't be as pronounced as when used dry, some interesting effects can be achieved.

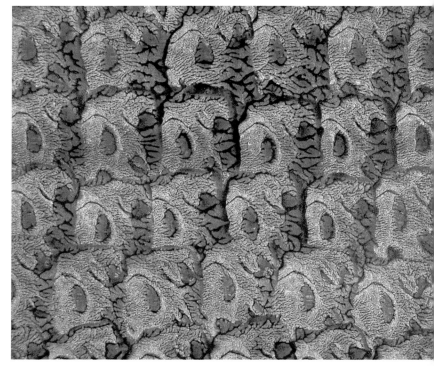

By using modeling clay to stamp in your paste, unusual images like this can be created. The darker areas were the result of depressions in the clay.

A paste-covered sheet of paper was repeatedly stamped with a crumpled piece of newspaper to create this design.

Making Prints in Paste

Hands and fingers (or feet, for that matter) can allow you to make your mark as a paste-paper designer. Then the sponge you use to clean yourself up can be used as a great printing tool, too!

MAKING FINGER AND PALM PRINTS

Although it's probably not a good idea to do a lot of "body printing," especially if you're using cadmium colors, which can be toxic, it's hard to resist working with such handy tools. Fingers and palms make wonderful textured designs. Results are immediate and foolproof—if you make your paste a little more liquid than usual and apply a generous amount of paste to create enough suction to raise the paste. This is like a return to kindergarten! And some of the images look quite sophisticated. Angels in the paste, anyone?

MAKING SPONGE PRINTS

Making sponge prints is another effective way to create an all-over pattern in paste.

Kitchen sponges, sea sponges, and makeup sponges will all leave interesting patterns as you dab them against your pasted paper, pulling off some of the paste and color. Look for sponges with large and small holes and in a variety of sizes to give yourself more patterning options. You can also enlarge some of the holes or make them more irregular by tearing out pieces of sponge to customize them. Use the sponges to stamp the sheet in a random manner, or be methodical in positioning your sponge to let the outline of the sponge be part of your design. Small rectangular sponges can be carefully placed to create a textured geometric pattern. By using just the edges of a kitchen sponge, pointed areas resembling mountains can be formed.

Purchase washed and cleaned sea sponges when possible; the unwashed variety contains sand and tiny shells that must be totally removed before use. Also, make sure you thoroughly rinse dish sponges before using them for patterning, as many contain a soap that will continue sudsing and cause bubbles to appear in your paste. Not a bad effect, really, but not predictable enough to use as a design tool.

You'll get a more interesting sudsy sponge print if you make your own concentrated mixture of dish detergent and water and dip your sponge in this before tapping it against your pasted sheet. The soap will remove more of the paste than using the sponge alone, and when the suds pop they'll leave little mottled areas in the design.

Try slightly wetting your sponge or coating several sponges with different colored pastes to create some interesting blurred designs on your sheet. Sponge printing and printing with crumpled paper and plastic can produce wonderful background images to combine with combed movements or other artwork and calligraphy.

Teaching by Jill Taylor. Jill often applies various colored pastes with sponges to create a colorful textured paste paper for her calligraphy and drawings. 11 × 17 in. (28 × 43 cm).

Creating Texture with Rubbing Plates

Plastic rubbing plates or stencils, often used with pastels or graphite pencils to add patterns to drawings, can create interesting textures in your paste. There are lots of patterns to choose from, including optical illusions, architectural patterns like brick and stone, and fabric textures. The plates are flexible enough to be easily pressed into a layer of paste and will leave a distinct impression when you peel it off the sheet. You can use them over and over by just rinsing them after use. Another way to use these plates is to place them under your paper, apply the paste, and then roll over the paste with a brayer. The depressions in the plates will allow more paste to accumulate and give a darker textured design—often a good starting point for additional paste designs.

Found objects—like chicken wire, pieces of berry baskets, and radiator screens with holes—can be used as found rubbing plates and will leave a textured image if you place it under your paper and roll over it after you apply the paste. Anything placed under your paper will leave a distinct impression when you brush over it, as you are bound to discover when a stray brush hair or bit of dried leftover paste appears and spoils the sheet you are brushing down. By the same token, however, you'll find that even something as thin as a paper cutout can be deliberately placed below the paper being coated with paste to leave a watermark-like impression in the paste.

A plastic rubbing plate and the design created when a paste-covered sheet, applied over it, was rolled with a brayer.

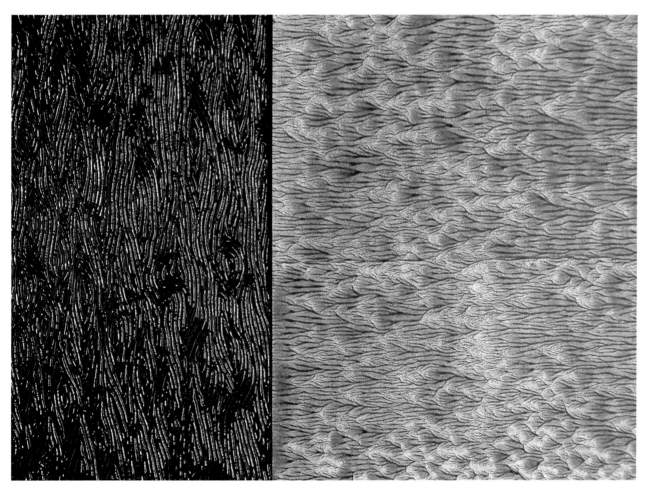

Making Brush-Textured Papers

Large or small, stiff or floppy, brushes are a delight to use to pattern a paste paper. You can use just brush strokes to create a design, or employ brushes in novel ways to create highly textured images: use the tip of the brush by holding it bristles-side down, or slap the entire side or edge of the brush into your paste to create feathery designs. Concentrate on repeating the same motion over and over to create a rhythm. Repeatedly slapping a brush against a pasted sheet sounds and feels great (especially after struggling to keep a tight scallop under control). It's fun to play wild drumming music when creating brush-print papers.

Cover a sheet with brush prints and then go over it a second time to make it look even more complex. When you've explored making brush-print papers by removing paste with each slap, try using brushes filled with colored paste to create subtle, multicolored brush-print designs. Brushes can be used to create undulating waved patterns in your paste, as well. Coarse bristles, like those made from broom straw, will leave a rougher design, while smooth-bristle brushes can be used to create circular swirls of colored paste, a moody accent to a paste-painted artwork.

A lacy design created by slapping a pasted sheet with the side of a brush.

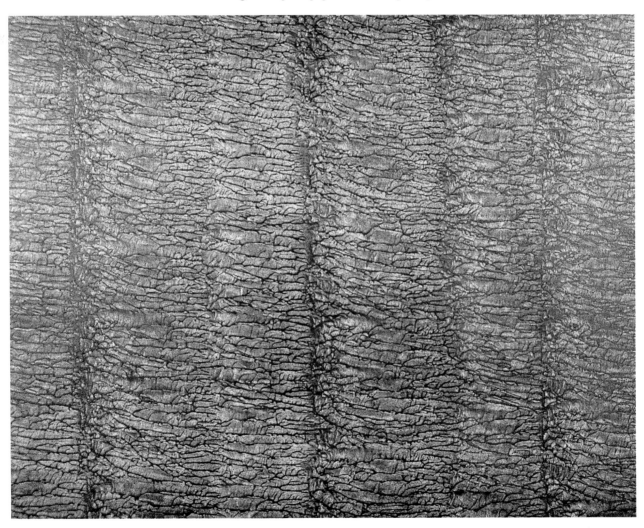

Paste painting by Nancy Culmone, from Southwest Wind *series. Brush strokes were used to convey the feeling of a swirling wind. 12 × 8¹/₂ in. (30 × 22 cm).*

Pulled Paste Papers

Amazing designs that resemble foliage can be created by coating two sheets of paper with paste, lightly pressing the papers together with your palms, and then slowly pulling them apart. The suction created causes the paste to rise into a network of ridges that resemble mosses, bushes, and tree-covered mountains.

Different effects can be achieved by using thick or thin pastes, by sandwiching string, felt, lace, or other materials between the pasted sheets, or by varying the amount of pressure applied to different parts of the sheet. You can coat your papers with the same color paste, or brush parts of one sheet with different colored pastes so that multicolored sheets will be created when the two sheets are pressed together. If the second sheet is brushed with a very wet paste, the color blends will be quite subtle as the wet colors mix together. Strips of cardboard, balsa wood, shaped cutouts, or leaves, also coated with paste, can be placed here and there on top of a pasted sheet and then removed to create feathery veined patterns in isolated parts of a paste paper.

The textured and blended designs on this book cover by Beth Beauchamp were made with pulled paste-paper techniques.

Creating Speckled Papers

Speckled papers can be made by making a thin colored paste and using it to spatter color over a pasted sheet. To spatter, use a stiff brush to brush your paste through a sieve, or lightly coat a small vegetable brush or toothbrush with color or colored paste. Holding the brush bristle-side up, with the front of the brush tipped down toward your paper, drag a ruler or tongue depressor toward you over the bristles. You may want to spatter outside or work within a cardboard box (with the front of the box removed), as the paste and paint will be broadcast over a wide area.

Another tool to use for this technique is the speckling brush made by Loew-Cornell. When you coat the brush tips with paint or thin paste and turn the handle, the brush rotates against a metal pin, spattering the color in the direction in which you turn the handle. It gives a more regular pattern than other makeshift tools. When spattering papers, it's best to begin spattering off the sheet of paper to make sure your brush isn't too loaded with color, which can cause great blobs of paint to fall (instead of the desired regular speckles). Practice by spattering closer or farther away from the surface of your paper to see how that affects the design.

Some found objects, like cut-flower stabilizers with metal spikes, or caps with plastic spikes for the feet of furniture, can be dipped in colored paste or paint and then pressed against the pasted sheet to distribute a series of dots of color. This will resemble spattering in isolated areas.

A speckled paper made by applying thinned metallic-colored pastes over a sheet previously patterned with a textured paint roller.

CHAPTER 4

Creating Roller and Brayer Prints

Rollers or brayers make great paste-paper tools and are perfect for producing collage materials. You can choose from an assortment of rollers including soft rubber, hard rubber, foam, and Lucite brayers. Rolling pins with and without decorative cut designs can also be used to create a continuous repetitive design in a paste-covered paper. You can use the rollers as is, carve them, or build up their surface to add to your design options.

OPPOSITE: Bali Dreams, *by Diane Maurer-Mathison. Hard rubber brayers were carved and rolled through thick paste to create the paste-paper elements in this collage. Paste paper, marbled paper, and handmade paper, 11 × 11 in. (28 × 28 cm).*

Creating Textured Roller Prints

By varying the thickness of your paste, the type of roller you use, and the amount of pressure you apply to the roller, you can create a variety of textured designs. I often roll out my paste carefully with an uncarved soft roller, minimizing the design the edge of the roller makes, to create a paper with a bit of texture, and then use combs over the texture to further enhance the sheet. If your paste is a little uneven, this technique will help to smooth it out as well. Another way to use an uncarved or undecorated roller is to apply more pressure and make wandering paths through the paste, letting the edges of the roller pattern the paper as it moves. Rollers of different widths can accentuate this type of design.

An unadulterated soft brayer was rolled through paste in several directions to create this design.

Cut Brayer Designs

If your design is cut intaglio, it will cause a depression in the surface of the roller. If you gouge out intaglio oval shapes in your brayer the following will happen: when the roller goes over the paste, the cut areas will print, remaining as paste-covered ovals when the roller material around them lifts the paste away. If the brayer is cut so that a relief or raised image is left, the area surrounding the relief will print or remain paste covered as the relief displaces the paste. Because there is less rubber to carve away, the intaglio image is usually easier to cut. But rollers that have a lot of rubber remaining sometimes slide a bit as you roll them through your paste and can create unexpected breaks in the patterning. Not a flaw, really, just an aberration. In fact, some paste-paper designers, like book artist Laura Wait, use this effect to advantage.

Designs cut or burned into rollers, along with rollers with built-up areas, can be used to create images in paste.

BELOW: *A photo album and slipcase covered in a roller-printed paste paper by Laura Wait.*

CUTTING AN INTAGLIO DESIGN INTO A BRAYER

The type of tool used to carve brayers depends upon the type of brayer you use, the intricacy of the design, and your experience using linoleum-cutting tools. If you've never used carving tools before, it's best to start out with a soft roller and a simple design. You may want to notch the roller repeatedly to remove parts of the rubber with a utility knife.

RIGHT: *A hard rubber intaglio-carved brayer and the design it produces.*

BELOW: *Using a linoleum cutting tool to carve a soft rubber brayer. The removable handle on a Ranger roller makes it possible to hold the brayer in a vise, which makes carving easier.*

Use a brayer that can be removed from its handle, like those made by Ranger Industries, if possible, and work slowly and carefully to avoid slipping off the roller and notching yourself. It's a bit trickier to carve material with a rounded edge than it is to cut into a flat piece of linoleum or board. With a little practice, you'll be able to carve rollers and even work on brayers that are permanently attached to a handle.

Laura Wait describes her technique for carving a hard rubber brayer:

> *The cut brayers I use for repeating patterns are hard rubber. It is much easier to cut these with crisp lines using a woodcutting or linoleum cutting tool. I first draw on the brayer with a ballpoint pen since its ink is shiny and I can see it over the dull black of the brayer. Then I carefully cut with the sharp tool. The rubber is not very thick, and you must try to avoid cutting through it in too many places or it will delaminate.*

If you're working with a soft, light-colored brayer, which is easier to cut than the hard rubber one Laura uses and, in my experience, seems to grip the paste better, you can draw your design on the rubber using a permanent pen and use the inked lines as a cutting guide. Ranger makes an assortment of different size rollers with removable handles that are easy to carve. You can buy the brayers without the handles, too, so that you can have a number of carved brayers in your paste-paper toolbox.

You can make a photocopy of a design from source material (I love using the ornament books showing designs from the art deco and art nouveau periods). Or trace the design with a soft graphite pencil, place it graphite-side down on your roller, and then use a burnisher to transfer the design to your roller. Using a piece of paper to determine the circumference of your roller will help you decide how large an image you can use effectively. Remember to make sure that the ends of the image you transfer to this paper match closely so that your pattern can repeat. Debra Tlach, whose brayer-carved designs are shown at right and at the bottom of this page, offers her technique for transferring an image:

> *Print out your design using a laser printer or make a photocopy of the design. Then tape your design onto your roller, securing the paper as tightly as possible against the rubber. Using a cotton ball dampened with nail polish remover containing acetone, gently dab the paper so that it is damp but not soaked. This will transfer the toner to the rubber. Now you can use linoleum cutters to carve a design into your roller.*

CREATING RELIEF DESIGNS ON A ROLLER

The same techniques described above can be use to carve away parts of the roller and leave a raised design that will create a print by displacing the paste as you roll your brayer across your paste-covered paper. Use the same method of transferring a design to your roller and be prepared to spend some time carving away all those portions of the roller that you need to prevent from making contact with the paper. The time spent will be well worth it, as carved relief designs can be very elegant.

INCISING BRAYERS WITH A WOOD-BURNING TOOL

Wood-burning tools, like those made by Colwood Electronics, offer an easy way to incise rollers. They come with various tips that heat up and are held like a pen to burn a design into the brayer. These amazing tools are nothing like the wood-burning tools from years ago. Very little pressure is needed—the "carving" is all done by melting the rubber.

The relief design on this soft rubber brayer leaves a distinct impression in the paste. This Ranger roller was carved by Debra Tlach.

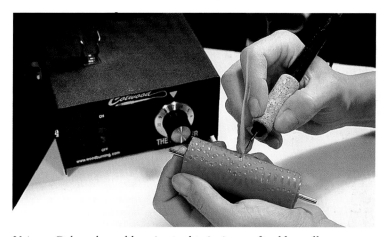

Using a Colwood wood-burning tool to incise a soft rubber roller.

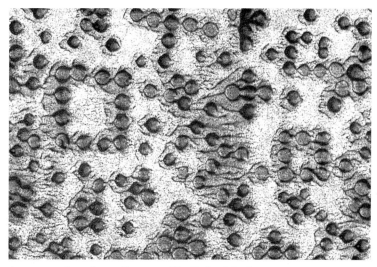

A print made with a roller incised by Debra Tlach.

Building Up the Surface of the Roller

An alternate way to create a relief image is to build up designs on the surface of the roller. Rubber bands or string can be wrapped around the roller to produce a pattern of meandering and intersecting lines as the roller moves forward. Lace or netting can be glued onto the roller for more patterning options. Unmounted rubber stamps, too, can be glued in place and used to create repeating prints in paste.

Pieces of Buttercut (described on page 44) can be pressed into place on the roller to make easy yet intricate relief designs. Try cutting strips of fuzzy Velcro for another self-adhesive addition to your roller. Play with all sorts of things to create texture in your work. Bubble wrap, felt, textured wallpaper, even flocked fabric can lend themselves as good roller printing materials. Even if the material you choose doesn't give you the anticipated results, you may make a valuable discovery along the way. For example, I recently placed several types of Velcro dots and lines on a roller to test whether the fuzzy or hooked surface would print better. In my haste, I left too much space between the Velcro dots, allowing the rubber to drop down to the surface of the paper as I rolled my brayer. The roller bumped along like a car with a flat tire but produced an image that I found perfect for winter snowscapes in my collages.

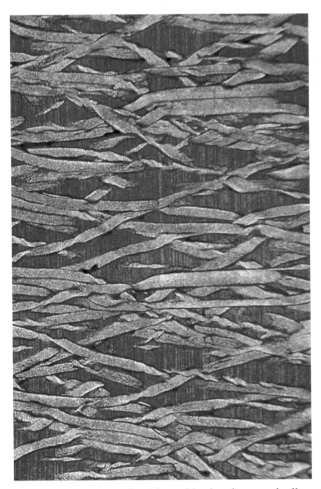

A paste-paper print made with a rubber-band-wrapped roller.

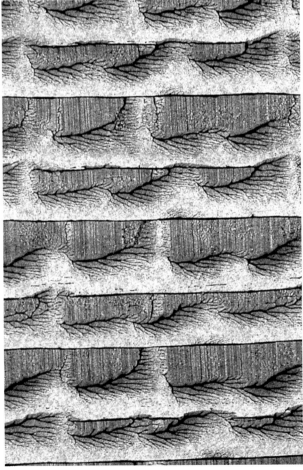

My "flat tire" print made with a roller wrapped in Velcro dots and strips.

Using Purchased Rolling Pins

Wooden rolling pins often wind up at flea markets and garage sales and can be purchased for very little money. The old-fashioned type, with handles that remain stationary as the center of the rolling pin moves, is the easiest to use. Buttercut is simple to attach to the rolling area, and, because the width of the rolling pin is larger than most brayers, you can cover more of your paper with each pass. Small spirals, geometric designs, or randomly placed short strips of material can create an effective all-over design. Rolling pins can also be wrapped with string or rubber bands.

Rolling pins with decorative relief and intaglio cuts are often sold in specialty kitchen stores. Developed for making decorative designs in cookies and pie crusts, they can be used to impart decorative designs on your paste papers. You'll have to brush on a rather thick coating of paste, however, to get the cut wood to print. Sometimes a rolling pin that looks spectacular yields a disappointing design, as only the highest point of the relief design will make contact with your paper and leave a mark in the paste. (Because cookie dough is soft and thick, the rolling pin can leave a better design in that material.) If the all-over design is not satisfactory, you can always use it as a background print for further embellishment with other paste-paper tools.

SUGGESTIONS FOR CREATING ROLLER-PRINTED PASTE PAPERS

Try some of the following techniques with your rubber and wooden rollers:

- Roll away from you in one direction and then move the roller slightly over to the right and reverse direction, rolling toward you.
- Roll horizontally over a vertical rolled pattern.
- Roll over a wet roller print with another cut roller to make a more complex design.
- Place dots of glue on a hard rubber roller, or use one of the commercially produced textured rollers to repeatedly roll over a paste-covered sheet.
- Fold a paste-covered sheet in half and then roll over it to create a mirror-image design.

A paste-paper print made with a textured roller.

A Rorschach print made with an uncarved roller.

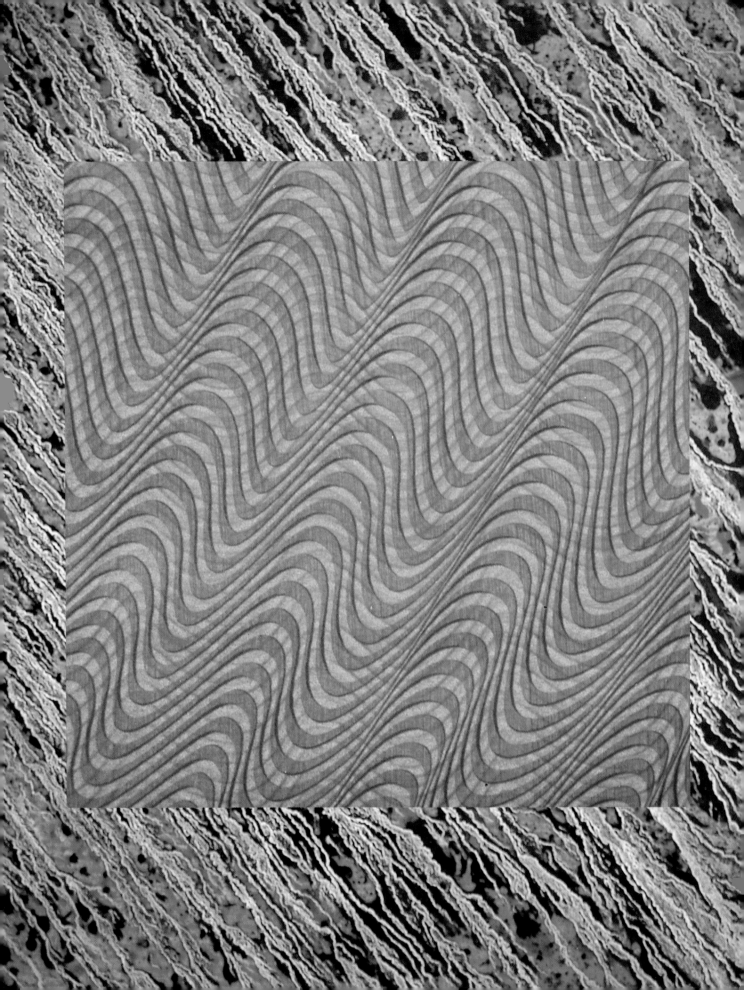

CHAPTER 5

Special Design Techniques

Creating designs in paste is a very freeing experience that tends to open us up to playful experimentation. Maybe it's because we are reminded of the fun we had with finger painting as children, or maybe it's because we know we can just brush over unsuccessful designs with another coat of paste and almost completely eradicate the evidence that we made such a clunky design. When you've made all the standard patterns in paste you'll probably start looking around for more patterning tools.

I sometimes fantasize about creating a large "transportation paper" by rolling a lawnmower, wheelbarrow, bicycle, and other large, wheeled objects over a paste-coated sheet, or having a bunch of friends wearing shoes with different treads walk through the paste. I'm sure you'll think of some of your own paste-paper experiments. In the meantime, here are some more ideas for increasing your design repertoire.

OPPOSITE: *A double-image waved paste-paper design. The elongated curves were created with a rubber graining comb.*

Combining Different Types of Designs

Although combs, stamps, rollers, and texturing tools can be used by themselves to produce exciting papers, it's great fun to gather all your tools and use several on one sheet to create combined designs. While some of the tools, like wooden stamps, may require a thicker application of paste, and some of the fine combs may work better with a thinner paste application, with practice you'll find a happy medium that will work for the tools you wish to use together.

One of the classic designs often seen on paste papers from the eighteenth century and still popular today is a paste design composed of a grid of large square or diamond-shaped blocks, with a small flower or bird stamped in the center of each diamond. The diamond pattern may be comprised of narrow combed lines made with a calligraphy pen or a potter's tool, or drawn with a chopstick. Where lines cross each other, each intersection may be marked with a tiny motif.

There are many ways to create motifs to be framed within a diamond pattern or other grid you've created on your paste paper. A wood-block or rubber stamp could be used to create

the design. Because it is so easy to carve, balsa wood or even a potato could also be fashioned into a bird, flower, or other shape and used to stamp an image in the center of a diamond pattern. A simple thumb print, often seen on historic paste papers, is another type of motif that can look interesting when repeatedly framed within a grid of intersecting lines.

Textured designs made with rollers or pulled-paper techniques create a beautiful background for combed designs done over them while the paste is still wet. The smooth lines juxtaposed with the nubby texture of the paste gives each sheet lots of contrast. I also like to spread paste on a strip of balsa wood and press it into wet paste to create a textured line to play against a background of layered, combed designs.

Look at some of the combined images shown to gain inspiration for your own designs. Then visit hardware stores, auto-supply stores, kitchen centers, and flea markets to fill the larders. Even pet-supply shops and toy stores can yield things that can be modified (a hamster wheel, for instance) to give you patterning ideas.

BELOW LEFT: *A stamped dragonfly motif within diamond-shaped areas is reminiscent of classical paste-paper designs. Rubber stamp by Rubber Stampede.*

BELOW RIGHT: *This meticulous paper by Eva Van Breugel is comprised of brushed, combed, and stamped designs.*

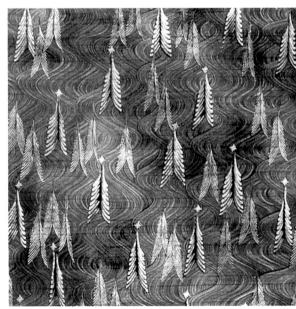

Drawing in the Paste

If you have drawing abilities or calligraphic skills, very elegant papers can be made by using a chopstick, a thin strip of balsa wood, or even a matchstick to create designs in paste. (Some paste artists swear by the flexible, pointed dental tools you can buy to stimulate your gums!) Simple repetitive representational images, like the tree branches shown at right, are easy to create, even if you don't have a refined drawing style or exceptional hand control. Practice similar curved lines by drawing them on a paper, and when you have mastered the gentle curves, attempt them in paste. Try using a broad-edged calligraphy pen held at a 45-degree angle to draw other designs in the paste.

To create this image, Jeff Mathison used a chopstick to draw branches in colored paste.

Important Things My Kids Taught Me. *Calligraphy on paste paper by Jill Taylor. 19 × 25 in. (48 × 64 cm).*

Creating Multiple-Image Designs

Although creating a design in the wet paste over another design technically constitutes making a multiple-image print, a much more interesting multiple-image design can be achieved by letting a patterned paste paper dry and then rewetting it, brushing on another color paste, and patterning the sheet a second time. Parts of the primary image will show through the second image when the patterning tool removes the second layer of paste applied.

If metal combs are used for a multiple-image print, you must be very careful not to tear the paper. Wetting the paper a second time often makes the first layer of paste a bit soft and the paper more fragile. It's best, if possible, to use rubber combs for this technique. If your favorite comb has metal teeth, try angling it as you draw it toward you to take some of the drag off the teeth.

Various colored pastes can be used for a second image. You can use contrasting colors or work in a similar hue to create a paper with a more subtle color change. I like working with metallics when creating

This striking box by Kelsey Woodward is covered in papers that are comprised of many layers of color and design. Photo by Jeff Baird.

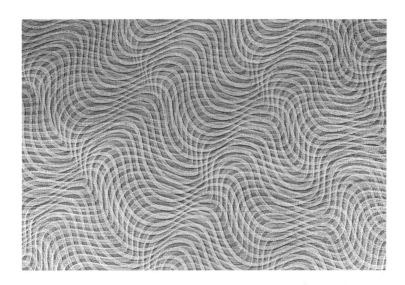

a second combed design. For my book projects, I often use a silver paste over a thalo blue primary image. Iridescent gold paste is a favorite over magenta or cadmium red combed papers with tight patterning.

By using combs with various tooth spacings, you can reveal more or less of your primary image and considerably change the paper design, even though your combing direction may stay the same.

Paste-paper artist Kelsey Woodward likes to create a paper that "gives the illusion of depth, mystery, and complexity." To achieve this, Kelsey often applies three layers of color and design. As she explains, "Each layer is applied using various techniques. The first layer may be a pastel color, a series of stripes in various colors, and/or an overall pattern created by additive or subtractive tools such as stamps, combs, etc."

You can also create a multiple-image design by brushing paste on a commercially printed or hand-decorated paper. I sometimes create paste designs over my marbled papers to use in collages. Applying paste over a block-printed paper is another way to create an interesting design with a lot of depth. The color and patterning will change dramatically, but the initial image will peek through your paste. Try brushing and patterning paste applied over a stenciled or rubber-stamped image to continue exploring the medium.

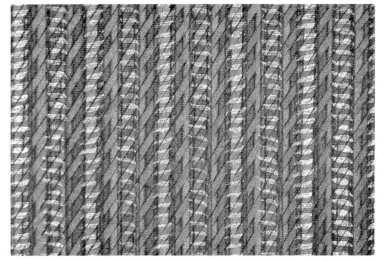

TOP: *A gold overlay of paste running across a previously made diagonal design creates a lively paste paper.*

CENTER: *A paper created by patterning paste that was applied over a block print design.*

BOTTOM: *Mimi Schleicher applied paste over one of her marbled works and combed through it to create this paper.*

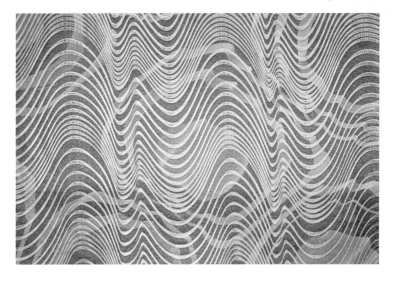

Creating Paste-Paper Underpaintings

Many paste artists create an underpainting as a way of beginning a design. Anne-Claude Cotty starts with an underlayer of rhythmic strokes drawn with Sennelier iridescent pastels, which shimmer through subsequent layers of colored pastes. She prizes the clean, bold effects achieved by using one tool—a plastic adhesive spreader with four different-size teeth.

Peggy Skycraft sometimes creates gridlike underpaintings by rubbing oil pastels over a rubbing plate and then applies colored paste over them. She and other paste-paper artists often use a wipe-out tool, like a potter's tool with a rubber tip, in a linear sweeping motion to remove wet paste and allow an underpainting to show through in a flash of color.

Iridescent pastel work shimmers through subsequent layers of colored paste in these accordion-fold books, Hummingbirds, by Anne-Claude Cotty. Anne-Claude relies on one tool—a plastic adhesive spreader—to create designs. 4 × 6 × 1 in. (10 × 15 × 2.5 cm) closed; 22 in. (56 cm) open.

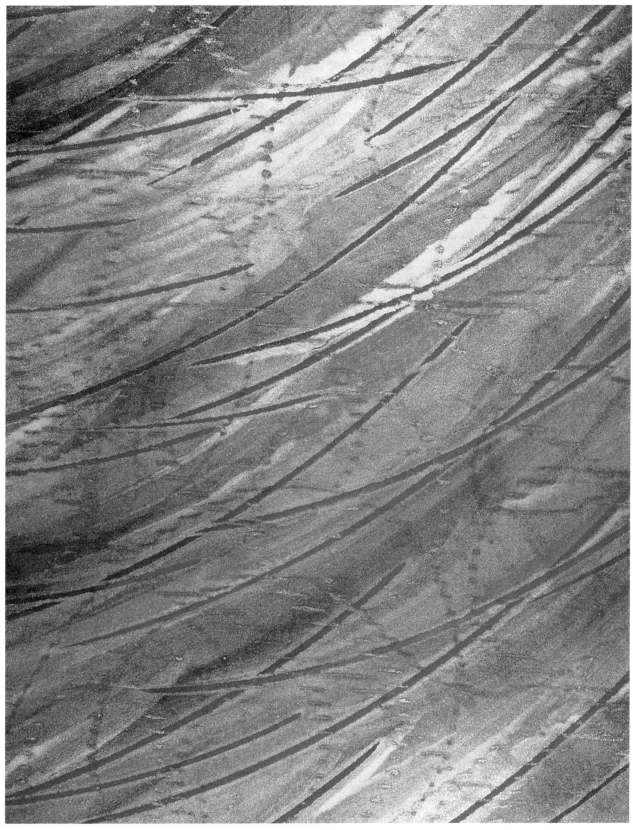

Peggy Skycraft often uses a wipe-out tool with a rubber tip to remove wet paste and allow an underpainting created with her oil pastels to show through.

Using Friskets and Masks

Friskets and masks may be used to block out parts of the paper being coated with paste. The mask will prevent the paste from reaching the area it covers. Some paste-paper designers apply a heavy paper or Mylar mask on the dampened sheet of paper and hold it in place

Frisket film cut in the shape of swallows was used to block out areas of a combed paste paper. When the sheet was coated with paste and patterned a second time, the isolated bird silhouettes remained.

Nancy Culmone uses masking techniques to create paste-paper backgrounds with a paste-paper border for her amazing calligraphic "letter portraits." From Ductus Divertimenti-Letter Portals. *Colored pencil calligraphy on paste-painted paper. 7 1/2 × 8 in. (19 × 20 cm).*

as they brush over it to deposit colored paste. This technique may work for simple rolled or brush-patterned designs; more complicated designs will require the use of frisket film. This art-supply product comes in sheets and rolls and, although a bit expensive, should give you good results.

You can usually use a high-tack frisket film on heavy papers being paste-painted and apply it before misting the paper with a spray bottle. Use an X-Acto knife and a metal-edged ruler over a cutting mat to cut out a simple geometric shape, like a triangle, from the film. Then peel off the backing, smooth it in place — adhesive side down — on your paper to be decorated, and, using a bone folder, rub or burnish the film in place. Pay special attention to the edges of the film where color tends to seep under. Although you can spray a fine mist to dampen the paper after the frisket is applied, this technique works best on heavy watercolor paper that won't wrinkle and so doesn't need to be wetted before painting.

For more detailed frisket work, draw an image onto the frisket film, use graphite paper to trace an image onto the frisket film, or use a rubber stamp. Although you'll get just a silhouette of the stamped image, it can lend an interesting accent to a paste-paper design. Uncomplicated designs, like the swallow pictured, can be cut with scissors. Images with tiny protrusions not only will be hard to cut but will be difficult to remove from the film's backing, so it's best to keep frisket work simple.

Masking techniques can be done on a blank sheet of paper to allow the paper color to show through as a silhouette image or on a previously pasted sheet so that when the mask is removed, the first layer of paste painting will be visible. This is a great way to create a paste-paper background with a secondary paste-paper border for artwork, as in the stunning piece by Nancy Culmone, pictured.

Using Mylar Stencils

Mylar stencils can also be used to mask out an area to be covered with paste. Multiple openings can be cut in a sheet of Mylar and placed over a sheet of paper that has been sponged down. Book artist Laura Wait, whose complex stencil work is shown at right, describes her techniques for cutting and using stencils:

I make my stencils out of 5-millimeter Mylar. They are usually cut to be larger than the paste paper being created. Each stencil has shapes cut into it. Because the cutting must be done carefully, I use a scalpel blade and a straight edge on top of a cutting mat, which gives more control. The blade must be very sharp and the Mylar dulls the blade quickly. I draw the shapes with a Sharpie pen. The shapes can be quite complicated, but are easier to use if they are simple—using a brush to apply the paste can easily abrade complicated shapes like stars and zigzags.

Laura describes her technique for creating the paper pictured:

This paper was made with a series of Mylar stencils. First the paper is sprayed and smoothed down. A layer of paste is added, and then the Mylar is placed on top and smoothed out. Paste was applied directly on top of the Mylar so that it goes into all the shapes. The paper is dried at this time. When new layers are added, I apply another layer of paste and then repeat the process. Interesting effects happen with all the layers. The interference paints are especially successful with this method, and the light colors shine best on dark backgrounds. I do not wash the backs of the Mylar between every paste paper. The residue of paste can make interesting color changes and textures when mixed with a fresh layer.

Although some paint may creep under stencils when the paste is applied, the soft-edged design can be lovely. Be sure to remove the stencil by pulling it straight up. Then try combing through the design to pull some of the color into the open areas for another type of image.

A unique paste paper created with a series of Mylar stencils by Laura Wait.

Using an Uncolored Coating of Paste

Some unique paste papers known as "dropped paste papers" were popular in Switzerland during the 1970s and 1980s. These were made by dropping various inks, wood stains, or watercolors on colorless paste. The reaction between the paste and the other coloring materials caused mosslike projections to extend from each spot of color, giving each paste-covered sheet a very unusual design.

In her research, Swiss paste-paper artist Virginia Passaglia found that several different techniques were used to create interactions between the paste and the colors applied. In some instances, color and oxgall (a strong surfactant used in marbling) were mixed together and then dropped on top of the uncolored wet paste. Another technique involved mixing potash into the paste before applying it to the sheet and then dropping color on top. Alum might also have been mixed into the color to create an unusual design when dropped on the paste. By putting the paste-covered sheet on a slanted base before applying the paints or inks, one could accentuate the designs formed by the chemical reactions and create a "trickled" paste paper as well as a "dropped" one.

Many contemporary paste-paper artists apply an uncolored coating of paste to a sheet before working on it. Nancy Culmone likes to cover a thick watercolor paper with a thin layer of clear paste and then go over this with layers of colors, working with a light touch so the two layers don't mix. Scraping or marking through the layers at once gives an exaggerated texture to her papers. She often uses pastels or watercolor crayons under or on top of translucent paste layers to create her paste paintings.

Paul Maurer uses a clear paste, sometimes mixed with acrylic medium to reduce drying time, to coat heavy paper for his paste-paper calligraphic drawings. He notes that a thick and thorough coating of paste enables him to work longer and get through to the paper surface and color. Paul likes to work in black and white, working quickly with minimal materials. While his uncolored paste is wet, he uses a brush to draw an image—a gesture, outline, or silhouette of a subject in acrylic color. Then he uses metal or plastic combs or calligraphy pens to swiftly pattern the images.

His step-by-step photos illuminate the unique way he creates his paste-paper drawings. The vibrant energy of his working methods is evident in his drawings and paste paintings shown on page 72.

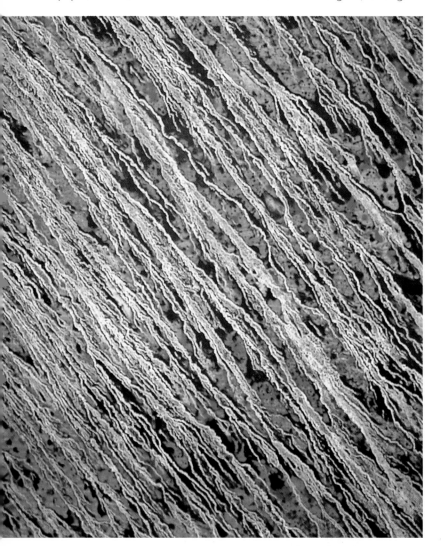

A "trickled" paste paper, France, 1970.

The Best Teacher
*by Nancy Culmone.
Nancy often uses
pastels or watercolor
crayons under or
on top of translucent
paste layers and
then scrapes through
all the layers of
wet paste at once to
create her paste
paintings. 13 × 20 in.
(33 × 51 cm).*

*Layers of stamping
and pastel coloring
mingle with split pen
and graining comb
paste-paper work
on this page from
Campo Santos, an
artist's book by Paul
Maurer. 11 × 17 in.
(28 × 43 cm).*

Paul Maurer applies acrylic color to a sheet of paper coated with uncolored paste to begin a paste-paper calligraphic drawing.

Paul Maurer using a metal graining comb to create patterns in the color supported by the paste.

A paste-paper drawing by Paul Maurer using the techniques demonstrated.

Mary Howe's Unique Technique

Mary Howe uses a technique somewhat similar to Paul Maurer's, but over a colored paste, and working not with a brush but a pipette. She fills a pipette with colored paste and then lays down a line of color on top of a sheet previously coated with a contrasting colored paste. Mary then manipulates the line into a spiral or combed design by using graining combs. Mary also uses the pipette to apply dots of colored paste to strategic areas of her papers. The dots and elongated lines and spirals of color appear here and there on a sheet, lending a playful quality to her work.

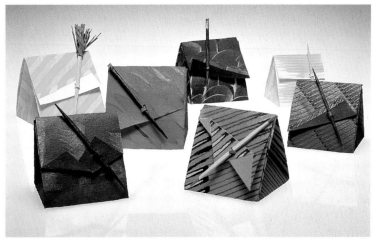

Folded Boxes *by Mary Howe. Mary's novel paste-paper techniques perfectly complement her spirited folded boxes. 2 1/2 × 2 1/2 × 2 1/2 in. (6 × 6 × 6 cm). Photo by Ken Woisard.*

Send in the Clowns *(detail) by Mary Howe. The dots, elongated lines, and spirals, which Mary creates by using a pipette to apply color, lend a playful quality to her work. A musical button plays the tune for which the work is titled. 4 1/2 × 8 in. (11 × 20 cm). Photo by Ken Woisard.*

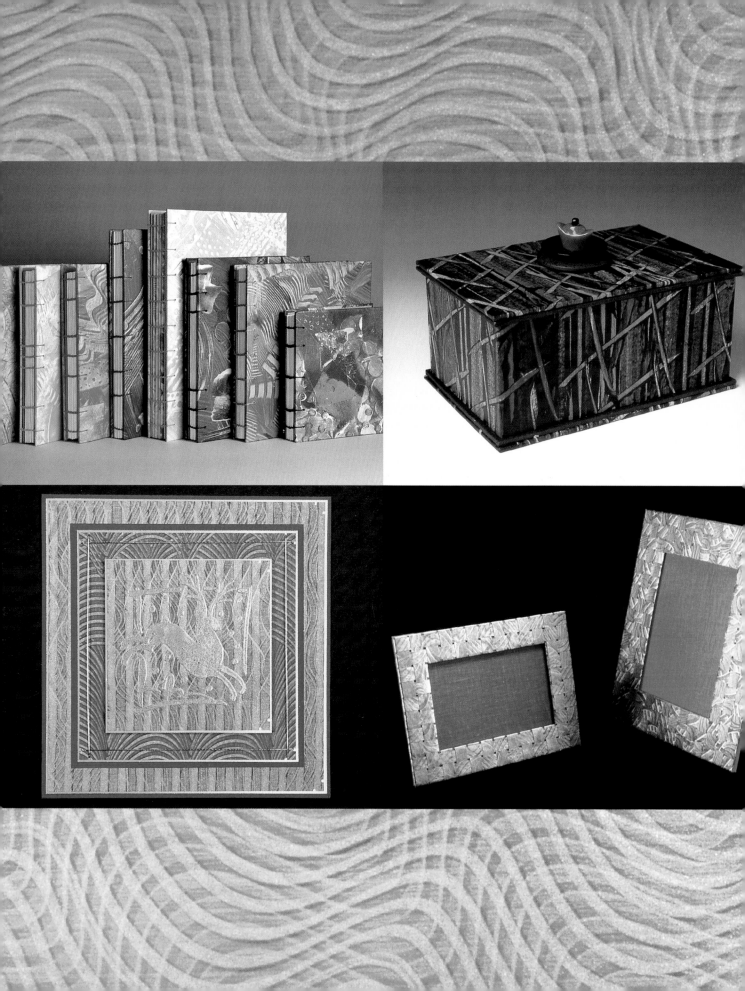

CHAPTER 6

Paste-Paper Projects

Paste papers have been used for centuries to decorate the covers and end-papers of books. Their allure is not diminished today; they share a prized place with other handcrafted papers on the covers and interiors of books created by book artists and small press publishers. But paste papers are no longer relegated solely to library shelves. Paste papers are now also being used to make beautiful art objects and graphic statements throughout homes and offices.

This chapter will show you how to use your paste papers to make some charming handmade books and functional objects like frames, boxes, and woven baskets that will add stunning decorative accents to a home or office. You'll also be able to modify projects and create new designs based on the paper art techniques you'll learn.

OPPOSITE TOP LEFT: *Handbound books with paste-paper covers by Beth Hale Beauchamp. Photo by Don Ross.*

TOP RIGHT: *Multiple layers of color and paste give Kelsey Woodward's button-topped boxes depth and beauty. Photo by Jeff Baird.*

BOTTOM LEFT: *Lea Everse transformed some of my ordinary cast-off papers into a beautiful layered card. Rubber stamp by Stampendous.*

BOTTOM RIGHT: *Myrna Bendett created paste papers with metallic acrylics and wove them together to make these picture mats.*

Preparation

By now you've probably tried some of the paste-paper techniques outlined in this book and discovered for yourself how varied the designs can be. Some of your papers will look sophisticated, while others may have a casual and playful quality about them. The papers may suggest uses for themselves, or you may start out with a project in mind and create a paste paper bearing a particular motif or color scheme to suggest the theme of a memory book you're making or complement a photograph you will frame in a paste-paper mat. Many book-arts, stationery, and home-decorating projects look spectacular in paste papers. Be sure to save the paper trimmings from these projects to make layered or woven cards. I sometimes send my paste-paper scraps and less successful papers to Lea Everse, an amazing card designer, who layers them with card stock and rubber-stamped images to create beautiful cards.

You might want to start saving up for some flat files or other paper-storage containers now, as you will no doubt soon have an array of gorgeous papers on hand that will need to stay protected until you decide how to use them. I usually separate papers by color, as my plans to keep them separated by size fell through long ago. In my house, any paste paper over 3 inches (8 cm) square gets saved. I quickly outgrew the flat files, and paste papers have now spilled over into my clothing drawers. (Not a big loss, anyway, as most of my clothes were covered with paste.) Always save a square of your favorite paste papers to remind yourself to go there again. And when you have a pile of these, try making a paste-paper scrapbook to document your paste-paper adventures.

EQUIPMENT

In addition to the materials and supplies used to create your paste papers, you'll need much of the equipment listed below to complete the wide range of paste-paper projects noted in this book.

SCRAP PAPER, WAXED PAPER, TRACING PAPER, AND SANDPAPER. Scrap paper will be placed under any papers being glued and should be replaced immediately after use to avoid getting unsightly glue marks on your finished project. I have found that an old phone book (tearing away pages that have a speck of glue on them) works just fine. When projects are being pressed, waxed paper will be placed over any areas that have been glued to prevent book pages or other parts of projects from sticking to each other. Tracing paper will be placed over a damp glued paper being burnished to prevent the bone folder or other burnishing tool from damaging it; scrap paper would also work, but it's nice to be able to see the paper you're burnishing to make sure it's all getting burnished flat. Sandpaper or an emery board will be indispensable for smoothing rough edges of book board.

BOOK BOARD. Book board, also known as binder's board or Davey board, is used to create rigid boxes and hard covers for books. Its thickness is described by a point system, with 90-point board one of the heaviest, measuring approximately $1/16$ inch (0.2 cm) thick. Thinner boards, like mat board, museum board, and other less expensive boards known as chip board, can also be used, depending upon the type of project you're making and whether you need to be concerned with using only archival materials. Art-supply and bookbinding-supply stores offer lots of choices. Although heavy boards require more patience to cut, they offer the benefit of being less likely to eventually warp. If your project isn't too large, a medium-weight board is usually heavy enough; it can be used for the box and book projects shown in this book. Although it is easy to cut, I don't recommend using foam board in projects because it is so easily dinged.

BOOK CLOTH. For a few of the projects you need book cloth. Get the paper-backed variety from a bookbinding supplier to make gluing easier.

ADHESIVES. Glue or paste will be the adhesive of choice for most of the projects. Double-sided adhesive film and other "dry adhesives" can also be used in some projects. I use mostly PVA or polyvinyl acetate glues, like Neutral pH Adhesive by Lineco Inc., Sobo, and "Yes" paste. The PVA glue dries clear, is flexible, and can be thinned with water. "Yes" paste, available at bookbinding and art-supply stores, is a mixture of wheat starch and glycerin. One benefit is the fact that it usually won't wrinkle even the thinnest papers. It dries quite quickly and can be thinned with water.

Another adhesive to try is the Daige Rollataq 300 Adhesive. This adhesive system features a 2.5-inch (6-cm) roller that lays down a clear, acid-free adhesive coating that stays repositionable for about ten minutes and then burnishes to a permanent bond.

Methylcellulose, wheat paste, and starch paste are other adhesives that may be used. Follow the instructions provided by the book-arts supply company for mixing and using them. For some projects, different adhesives, such as PVA glue and methylcellulose, can be mixed together so that the best qualities of each can be obtained. This will be especially important when looking for an adhesive that has high tack, yet is slow drying. A word of caution: rubber cement should never be used, as in just a few years it will bleed through papers and ruin them.

If you are concerned about creating projects that are archival, always check to make sure that the glues, as well as the papers and paints, are acid-free or pH neutral. If you need to add water to thin a glue, be sure to use distilled water to preserve archival properties.

CORDS AND RIBBONS. Most any strong and non-stretching ribbon or cord can be used to make an album or memory book, or to gather the pleats of an accordion-folded lamp shade. Bookbinding-supply houses, fabric shops, and jewelry-supply catalogs offer lots of decorative braids and cords.

NEEDLES. Bookbinding or weaving needles with eyes big enough to carry thin cords and ribbons will be needed for some projects.

PAPER CUTTER. If you have access to a large paper cutter—preferably with a bar to hold paper and board in place so that you can cut it without having the material slip—you can easily divide sheets of paper and lightweight board used in projects.

Some of the tools used to create paste-paper projects.

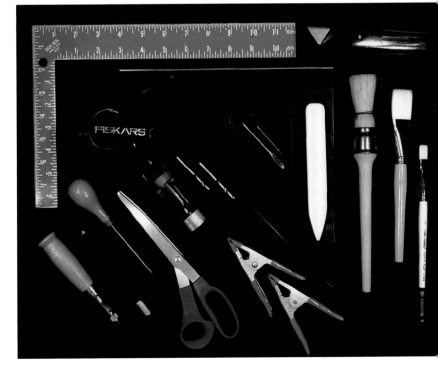

CRAFT KNIFE AND METAL RULER. If you don't have a paper cutter, you can make accurate paper cuts by using an X-Acto knife and a metal straightedge or steel square to guide the blade. Heavy chip board or Davey board should be cut with a mat or utility knife. Stock up on blades, and always use a sharp one to make clean cuts.

SMALL SQUARING DEVICE. Although a steel square will be indispensable for squaring and cutting book board, a plastic triangle or small T-square will come in handy when cutting short strips of paste papers, for scoring and folding papers, or to use as a guide when making book pages. One of my favorite tools is a plastic triangle with calibrations and grids for measuring and squaring, made by the C-Thru Ruler Company. The grid on this wonderful tool can be read on dark or light paper, and the triangle has a metal edge for cutting, too. I own five of these, with four carefully stashed away, just in case the company ever stops making them!

CUTTING SURFACE. A self-healing cutting mat or piece of glass with the edges taped should be placed under the paper or board being cut. Don't try to use cardboard as a cutting surface—it rapidly dulls knife blades.

SCISSORS. Although most cutting will be done with knives, various types of scissors, with long blades and short decorative blades, will come in handy.

CLAMPS OR CLIPS. These will be used to hold materials in place when holes are being made through book covers and pages.

HOLE PUNCHES. Various types of paper punches can be used in projects. A Japanese screw punch with different size bits is a great tool. When you apply pressure on the handle, it rotates the bit, creating a hole in the paper or board. Look for these in bookbinding-supply catalogs. Hardware-supply hole-punch sets can also be used for paper and board. Pound them with a rubber mallet to punch through a material to a rubber cutting mat. Awls, drill presses, and handheld drills, like the Craft Hand Drill, made by Fiskars®, can also be used to make page and cover holes for books.

AWL OR LARGE WEAVING NEEDLE. In addition to making holes in lightweight board and paper, an awl will be helpful for scoring papers to be folded for lamp shades and book pages.

BONE FOLDER. A bookbinder's bone folder is used for folding, scoring, and creasing papers. It is also used to press out air bubbles and wrinkles when gluing papers to other surfaces.

GLUE BRUSHES. Purchase a few large and small glue brushes to use, depending upon the size of your project. A large brush is necessary when applying glue to a large area of a cover board, but a small brush will be much more convenient for coating a thin strip of paper to be turned over a board to make a neat box corner. I find that slightly stiff, flat, synthetic-bristle brushes from art-supply stores work best for most jobs.

DAMP SPONGE. Always keep a damp sponge nearby when working with liquid adhesives. It will help remove glue from your fingers before it gets transferred to your papers and board.

BOOK PRESS. Two smooth boards and a few heavy books or bricks can be used to create a makeshift book press to prevent glued materials from warping as they dry. For small projects, just some heavy books will do the job.

BASIC PAPER-CRAFT TECHNIQUES

If you don't have much experience creating paper-craft projects, practice some of the techniques below to familiarize yourself with them before attempting them on your paste papers and boards. Although the techniques may seem alien at first, after you've done them a few times, they'll become second nature to you. A basic tenant of woodworkers holds true for paper artists too: always measure twice and cut once.

Finding Paper Grain

Book board and most machine-made papers have what's known as a "grain" or direction in which the fibers align themselves. Papers with the fold line running parallel to the grain of the paper will crease easily, without cracking, and hold their shape. Papers folded against the grain will crease unevenly, crack, and be generally uncooperative.

In constructing scrapbooks, boxes, covered mats, and other projects that are comprised of paste papers glued to boards, it will be especially important to note and keep track of the grain direction of your materials. Wet papers tend to curl with the grain, so it's important, when gluing them to each other or to book board, to make sure that the grain direction of both materials matches. If materials with opposing grain directions are glued together, they'll pull in opposite directions as they dry and create a warped project.

To test for grain direction in a sheet of paper, bend the sheet in half. If the paper easily collapses in on itself, you're bending with the grain. If the paper resists your efforts, you're bending cross grain. Test the paper in each direction and then pencil an arrow on it to mark the grain direction.

To test for grain direction in book board, hold the long edges of the whole sheet in your hands and attempt to bend it. Little resistance

means the grain is running parallel to your arms. Considerable resistance means you're bending across the grain. Pencil an arrow on pieces of book board as you cut them so you don't lose track of the grain direction. Because they don't bend easily, it's more difficult to test small pieces of heavy board.

Cutting Papers and Boards

There are several ways to cut papers and boards. The easiest way to make straight cuts is with a good-quality paper cutter. If you plan to do much work with heavy book board, creating rigid boxes or hardcover books, it makes sense to invest in a good cutter with a bar to assist you in holding material in place while you lower the chopping arm. An excellent choice would be the Kutrimmer. It comes in a floor or table model and will easily cut through book board. It costs several hundred dollars, however, and care must be exercised in using this type of cutter, as the blade will remain very sharp.

Most heavy mat board and book board is too thick to be cut on a moderately priced paper cutter. It can usually be divided more easily with a mat cutter (and a stock of sharp

Testing for paper grain. If a paper collapses easily when you attempt to bend it, you're bending with the grain. If it resists, you're bending cross-grain.

BELOW, TOP: *Using a utility knife and a metal square to slice through book board. Be sure to use a sharp blade.*

BOTTOM: *Scoring paper to prepare it for folding. A light touch properly indents the sheet; exerting too much pressure will break its surface.*

blades) or by using a utility knife and sliding a fresh blade against the edge of a metal ruler. Work over a self-healing cutting mat or a piece of glass with edges taped, and be prepared to make several cuts to cleanly divide your material.

Use an X-Acto knife to slice through paste papers or paper-backed book cloth in the same way. Hold the knife upright, and make sure you change blades often so that cuts are clean, not ragged. Rotary paper trimmers can also be used to cut lightweight papers, or papers can be cut with edging scissors to produce a decorative cut edge.

Scoring and Folding

Scoring, using a bone folder, awl, weaving needle, or other tool to crease a paper's surface, prepares a paper for folding. Your fold lines will be sharper and neater if you slowly and carefully score pages to be folded. Folding with the grain of the paper is recommended. To score, hold a C-Thru triangle, metal triangle, or other squaring device against the desired fold line, and, using the triangle to guide you, drag the point of the scoring tool down the length of the tool. The object is to indent but not break the surface of papers to prepare them for folding. Then bend away from, not into, the fold lines to crease them.

Working with Adhesives

The decision of whether to use an archival glue, paste, a glue stick, or an adhesive film to bond papers and fabrics will depend upon what kind of project you're working on and its intended life span. Spray adhesives and adhesive films, like Cello-Mount, will make your work go faster. Some adhesives will produce a weaker bond, however, so read labels carefully.

When working with liquid glues, try to work as quickly as possible to avoid having one area of the paper or board dry while you're working on another. Always work over a sheet of scrap paper (with lots more at hand) when applying glues, and work from the center toward the edges, spreading the glue evenly over the entire surface of the paper or board. Although some book and box artists like to glue an entire sheet of paper and then lay the book board on the glued sheet, I find it much easier and neater to apply the glue to the book board and brush on more glue when it is time fold over the edges of the paper or book cloth to adhere them to the book board.

Most of the directions in this book will call for using this technique, although you

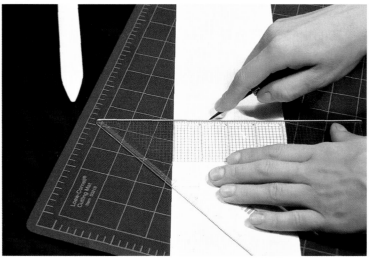

can try the alternate method and see which you prefer. I've found that applying glue to the board lessens problems with paper wrinkling—especially for novice bookbinders and paper artists. (It also lessens the likelihood of glue transferring to your fingers and onto your finished project.)

A number of double-sided adhesive films on the market today can also be used for projects. Some, like Cello-Mount, consist of a thin sheet of adhesive film sandwiched between two slippery protective papers. To use it, you peel away one protective sheet, exposing the adhesive, and apply your board or paper to it. When you peel away the other protective sheet, you're left with a sticky-backed piece of book board or paper.

Other mounting adhesives, like those made by Stick-Ease or Neschen, consist of a roll of very thin adhesive coated onto a release paper. Because this type of adhesive is not double sided, it's a bit trickier to work with. But its adhesive properties are great. And the Gudy-870 Mounting Adhesive from Neschen is acid- and solvent-free.

These products come with tips for using them and the suggestion that you practice working with them before using them on a project. It's best to practice procedures with any adhesive film product. When you're working with a liquid glue or Rollataq adhesive, there's a window of opportunity during which you can shift your book board and other materials into position should you miss the mark when you apply the adhesive to the paper. If your book board is backed with a *dry* mounting adhesive that is not repositionable, you get only one chance!

Burnishing

Burnishing is an important step in helping to create a good bond between glued boards and the papers that cover them. After your book

board has made contact with the paper that will cover it, turn the board over so that the paper faces up, and, working from the center outward, hold the bone folder on its side and push out any wrinkles or air bubbles that may be present. To avoid damaging a textured or fragile paste paper, work over a piece of tracing paper or other lightweight paper. Burnish bonds made with adhesive release papers, too, as air bubbles can also weaken them.

Burnishing will also aid you when folding scored papers. It can help you make sharp creases, which can give a neater appearance to all folded papers and help accordion-folded works open, close, and stand correctly.

Pressing

Papers and fabrics that have become wet with glue tend to stretch at first and then shrink back as they dry. This process can cause the book boards they cover to warp. To prevent warping, be sure to dry any projects made with wet adhesives under pressure. Interleave any wet areas with waxed paper to prevent glue from seeping out. A professional book press is the perfect means of applying pressure to make sure that paper art projects dry evenly, but a couple of flat, smooth pressing boards with heavy books or bricks on top will suffice.

Burnishing a sheet of paste paper to help it bond to the board below it. Tracing paper is placed over the decorative paper to protect it during the process.

Accordion-Fold Paste-Paper Sampler

MATERIALS

- Book board to create the hard covers
- Cutting tools: a utility knife and a metal square or professional paper or board cutter
- Pencil
- Sandpaper or an emery board (to sand the edges of rough book board, if necessary)
- Lightweight to medium-weight paste paper
- PVA glue
- Large and small glue brushes
- Scrap paper
- Tracing paper (optional)
- Bone folder
- Scissors
- Waxed paper
- Cover-weight paper for the interior pages (Canson Mi-Teintes works well)
- Long metal ruler or yardstick for cutting pages (omit if you have a large paper cutter)
- Awl or weaving needle for scoring pages
- Squaring triangle or ruler (with metal edge, if possible)
- Ribbon or cord to tie the book closed (optional)
- X-Acto knife
- Paste-paper samples or other material to place in your book

A simple accordion-fold or concertina book is a great place to house samples of some of your favorite paste papers. A design of Eastern origin, the book is really just one long piece of folded paper enclosed between two covers. Because the pages can expand, the book is capable of holding paste-paper memorabilia, like small combs or notes about creating designs, as well as paste-paper samples on both the front and the back of its folded pages. It makes a great gift for a friend who wants to see what your collection of oddball combs and implements can produce. Referring to the book months or years later can help jog your memory to remind you of patterns worth repeating.

The interior pages will be made from a heavy cover stock, with pages nearly as tall as the covers, so the book can stand open for display on a mantel or sideboard in your home and serve as a beautiful decorative accent as well as something useful. Someday I will create separate books for my favorite combed, pulled, and stamped papers.

CUTTING THE COVER BOARDS

Decide what size you'd like your book to be (mine is $3^7/8 \times 4^1/4$ inches [10 × 11 cm]) and then transfer the measurements to a piece of book board. Make sure that the grain of your board runs vertically. Use a utility knife and a square or a professional paper cutter to cut out front and back cover boards. Check to be sure that the corners are cut at right angles and that edges are straight. A "little bit off" can really stand out, ruining a completed project. If the cutting has left ragged edges on your board, gently sand them. Lightly pencil a line noting the grain direction on your cover boards.

The accordion-fold paste-paper sampler.

PREPARING THE COVER PAPERS

Determine grain direction on the paste paper you've chosen to cover the book boards. Arrange it on your worktable so that the grain matches your book board, and then cut two pieces, each 1½ inches (4 cm) wider and longer than the book covers. This will allow for a ¾-inch (2-cm) border around each cover board. Place each board in the center of the back of the paste paper you just cut and lightly trace positioning marks to help you gauge where to place the board when you glue it down. (After you have gained experience, you can omit this last step.)

GLUING THE BOARDS IN PLACE

Prepare to apply glue to the front cover by placing it on a sheet of scrap paper. Working from the center outward, brush on a thin layer of glue. Then place the cover glue-side down within the positioning marks on your paste paper. Immediately discard the scrap paper and wipe any glue from your hands before turning the paste paper and attached book board right-side up. Place a piece of tracing paper over the paste paper to protect it, and, using a bone folder, work from the center of the board outward to burnish out any air bubbles or wrinkles.

MITERING CORNERS

Mitering refers to the way that papers are cut or folded, fitted together at the corners of the boards they cover, and glued in place. Well-mitered corners are the mark of a good craftsperson. It pays to practice this operation a few times, as a poor mitering job can ruin an otherwise attractive work. You'll use this procedure in several of the other projects, so your practice will pay off.

After burnishing, turn the paper over again onto a clean piece of scrap paper so that the book board is again facing up. Miter the

A

B

C

corners by cutting off the corners of the paste paper, leaving about ⅛ to ¼ inch (0.3 to .6 cm) between the edge of the board and the end of the paper (see **step A**). Generally, twice the thickness of the book board is a sufficient margin of paper to cover the board corners. Apply glue to one long edge of paper (see **step B**), running the brush against the lip of the book board as you work, and fold the flap of paper over the book board to glue it down. (I like to stand the book on its edge for a moment and then lower it until it is flat, to press the flap of paper down, as in **step C**.)

D

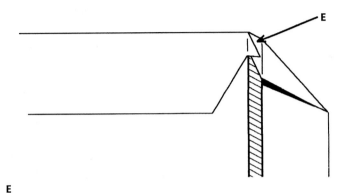

E

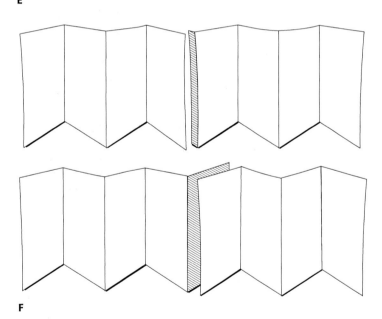

F

step **E**) that appears when the long edges of the paper are folded over. This overlap of paper, the result of leaving the $^{1}/_{4}$-inch (0.6-cm) space between the paper and the board, will prevent the corners of the book board from showing when the short flaps of paste paper are folded over. When the overlaps are tucked in place (angled slightly toward each other), apply glue to the remaining short paper flaps, fold them over, and burnish them in place. If you have difficulty positioning the glued flaps, you may find that prefolding flaps before applying glue makes the job easier.

Repeat these directions to cover the other piece of book board. Then sandwich the covers between pieces of waxed paper to keep glue from reaching other surfaces, and press the boards while you prepare the folded pages.

CREATING THE ACCORDION-FOLDED PAGES

Determine the height of the pages by measuring the height of your cover and subtracting $^{1}/_{4}$ inch (0.6 cm). This will provide a $^{1}/_{8}$-inch (0.3-cm) margin allowance around the endpapers when they're glued to the book covers. (A narrow margin is necessary if you want the book to stand open to display your paste papers.) Then measure the width of the cover and subtract $^{1}/_{4}$ inch (0.6 cm) to determine the width of each accordion-folded page.

CUTTING THE PAGES

Use a large paper cutter or a utility knife and a rule to cut a long strip of cover-weight paper for the pages of the album. The grain of the paper should run vertical, parallel to the vertical fold lines, and the width of the paper strip should match the measurement you chose for the height of the pages. Don't worry about the length of the paper—you can cut several strips and join them later to make a book with long folded pages (see step **F**).

Use your thumb and then the bone folder to smooth the edge of the cover paper against the side of the book board (see **step D**). Burnish the paper down so that it has no wrinkles, air bubbles, or loose edges.

Now glue down the other long paste-paper flap and burnish it smooth. Use your index fingernail or the tip of the bone folder to tuck in the small overlap of paper (labeled E in

FOLDING THE PAGES

Prepare to fold the pages by measuring off each page width for the entire length of the paper strip and making a faint mark with the tip of your awl or a needle. Place your squaring triangle at every other mark and score the paper by lightly running an awl or weaving needle against the edge of the squaring device. Then turn the paper over and score the remaining pages on the opposite side of the paper. Use your bone folder to crease the paper (away from the indentation) to create the first page of the book. Keep accordion-folding until you reach the end of your paper, making sure that the top and bottom edges of the paper always line up. To add pages to your book, join similarly folded pages together, as shown in **step F**. Finish your page strip by cutting off any excess that's not wide enough to be used as a page or that folds in the wrong direction.

ASSEMBLING THE BOOK

Assemble the book by brushing glue on the ends (endpapers) of your folded stack of pages and positioning them within the book covers so that a $^1/8$-inch (0.3-cm) margin surrounds them (see **step G**). Use your bone folder over a sheet of tracing paper to burnish the endpapers down. Insert a sheet of waxed paper between the covers and the first and last pages of the book to keep any excess glue from penetrating, and press the book until dry.

ADDING RIBBON TIES

If you wish to add ribbon ties to your accordion-fold book, do so—before the endpapers are glued in place—by laying down a thin line of glue across the inside of the back cover and pressing ribbon (or another material) into the glue. When extended around the back of the folded pages and over the front cover, the left side of the ribbon should be long enough to tie to the end that extends from the right side of the back cover.

APPLYING YOUR PASTE-PAPER SAMPLES

Decide upon the size and shape of the paste-paper samples that you want to apply to your book pages. An easy way to make triangular-shaped paper samples is to cut out a square of paper and then, using a metal-edged ruler and an X-Acto knife, slice the paper from one diagonal point to the other.

You can fill the book completely with paste-paper samples, or alternate pages with notes on how you made the papers. Using a dry adhesive will make this job easier. If you want to adhere actual combs or other paste tools, you'll need to use a heavy-duty adhesive made to bond the type of material you're including. The accordion-fold book structure is very versatile: you can make it large or small, in a horizontal or vertical format, and with or without rigid covers.

G

TIP

An alternate method of folding, which goes much faster, can be accomplished by measuring and scoring for the first fold and then turning the paper over and using the first folded page as a guide to determine where to score and fold the next. If you keep turning your paper over, make sure the tops and bottoms of your pages line up and you always use the *previous* fold as a guide. You may find, as I do, that this method works perfectly and that page size remains constant without expanding throughout your folding. Although this method is frowned upon by many and deemed impossible by some, it's worth a try. You, too, may find you have a hidden talent for it!

Flag Book

The flag book is a charming project that holds surprises between its covers. Instead of conventional pages, the book has an accordion-folded center spine on which strips of paper are adhered so that when the ordinary-looking cover is opened, many flags pop out at you in opposing directions. Humorous quotes or birthday greetings could be written on the flags to create a gift book. In addition to the paste design, stamping and cut work can accent the pages to make the book even more exciting.

The book could be made with hard covers like the previous book or, like the one pictured, be a soft-cover book made out of heavy paper or tag board that will fold without cracking and stand well on its own. If you make a book out of tag board and use a rather thin paste, you may be able to skip the process of prewetting the paper for paste designs. Kimberly Byerly, whose book is shown below, uses a very liquid paste that she often "drizzles on with a spoon" and then brushes over the paper. At any rate, be sure to avoid a heavy buildup of paste on the board that might crack when the paper is folded.

A paste-paper flag book by Kimberly Byerly.

Most of the following directions and diagrams are based on those provided by Kimberly Byerly.

CUTTING THE PAPER

Cut an 18- × 24-inch (46- × 61-cm) sheet of paper or tag board according to the diagram shown below.

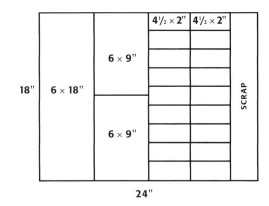

CREATING THE ACCORDION SPINE

Using a bone folder, crease the long strip of paper in half and then fold in each end to meet the center fold. You will have folded the paper in quarters. Next, accordion-fold the center two panels by creasing one fold to the next; then go back and crease between the folds until you have made a total of nine creases. When you view the accordion spine from the inside of the book, where the flag pages will be attached, you'll see four mountain folds and three valley folds, as shown. Adjust any folds going in the wrong direction.

A

B

An Alternate Method

Some papers are difficult to fold neatly without scoring them first. Others will crack if you score them on the incorrect side and then attempt to "reverse" the fold. If you find the previous technique problematic, try scoring your paper with an awl on the appropriate side before accordion-folding it.

To do this, with the front of the paper facing you, fold it in half. Now flip the paper over and, working on the back of the paper, measure out 2¼ inches (6 cm) from the right side of the center score line (which is a "mountain fold" when viewed from the back) and make a depression in your paper with the tip of the awl. Measure out another 2¼ inches (6 cm) from the previous mark and make another depression to indicate where to score. Do the same on the left side of the center score line. Score the paper on the back of the project at each mark. Then flip the tag board over so that the front faces you.

To score on the front side of the paper, mark off the four lines that will fall between the previous folds at 1⅛-inch (3-cm) marks. Score and then fold the accordion "spine" of your flag book. All your folds will be going in the correct direction and the spine should easily fall into pleats.

CREATING AND ATTACHING THE COVERS

Take the two 6- × 9-inch (15- × 23-cm) pieces, which will become your covers, and fold them in half so that the "good" side is facing out. Apply glue or dry adhesive around the inside edges of your folded cover, and attach the covers to the ends of the accordion-folded spine (see **step A**).

CREATING THE FLAG PAGES

The paste-paper flag pages are mounted on opposing sides of the mountain folds that appear when the book is opened. Eight 2- × 4½-inch (5- × 11-cm) flags will be adhered to the left-hand sides of the accordion folds. These will swing open to the right when the book is opened. Four slightly more narrow 1¾- × 4½-inch (4- × 11-cm) flags will be mounted on the right-hand sides of the folds and will swing to the left (in between the wider flags) when the book is opened. Trim the center row of flags and embellish all flags with stamp art or cut work, if desired.

GLUING THE FLAG PAGES IN PLACE

To prepare for gluing the flags in place, measure and mark 1⅛ inches (3 cm) into each flag (the width of each side of the mountain folds) so you know where to apply the glue or dry adhesive. Adhere the larger flags to the left sides of the accordion spine, lining them up with the top and bottom edges of the book. Then glue the narrow flags in place on the right-hand side of each mountain fold, making sure that they are placed in such a way as to swing through the other pages when the book is opened (see **step B**).

Hardcover Stab-Bound Scrapbook

MATERIALS

- Book board
- Pencil
- Cutting tools: a utility knife and a metal square or professional paper or board cutter
- Paper-lined book cloth
- PVA glue
- Large and small glue brushes
- A ¹⁄₈-inch to ¹⁄₄-inch (0.3- to .6-cm) strip of Plexiglas, cardboard, or balsa wood (to use as a spacing device between cover pieces; optional)
- Scrap paper
- Scissors
- Bone folder
- Lightweight to medium-weight paste papers for wrapping the book covers
- Metal-edged ruler
- Text-weight paste paper or plain paper for lining the covers
- Waxed paper
- Cover-weight paper for the text pages and page spacers
- Glue stick (optional)
- Clamp to hold pages in place for hole drilling or punching
- Hole-drilling/punching equipment: a hand drill, electric drill, screw punch, or punch and mallet
- Non-stretching ribbon or cord
- Awl or needle-nosed pliers to pull ribbon through stitching holes

Although this project has considerably more steps than the previous projects, it is not difficult to make. The results of your labor will be well worth the effort, too. This structure will make a very sturdy album that will last for years without showing wear. It features book cloth on the hinge area of the book (which takes most of the abuse of opening and closing) and hard covers wrapped in paste papers.

CUTTING THE BOOK BOARDS

Determine the shape and size of the scrapbook you'd like to create, make note of the vertical grain direction, and then cut four pieces of book board: two pieces for the front and back covers and two hinge pieces. The hinge boards are usually at least one inch (2.5 cm) wide. Make yours as wide as desired to coordinate with the size of your book. The book pictured has dimensions of 6³⁄₄ × 8³⁄₈ inches (17 × 21 cm) overall. The covers are comprised of hinge boards that measure 6³⁄₄ × 1¹⁄₄ inches (17 × 3 cm) and front and back cover boards that measure 6³⁄₄ inches × 7 inches (17 × 18 cm). The two boards that make up each cover have a ¹⁄₈-inch (0.3-cm) gap between them that allows the book to open. (You can make this book with one hinged cover and a one-piece back cover, if you prefer. Just be sure to add this ¹⁄₈-inch [0.3-cm] gap to the overall width of the back cover.)

CUTTING THE BOOK CLOTH

Cut two pieces of paper-backed book cloth each 1¹⁄₂ inches (4 cm) taller (to allow for a ³⁄₄-inch [2-cm] turnover) and 2 inches (5 cm)

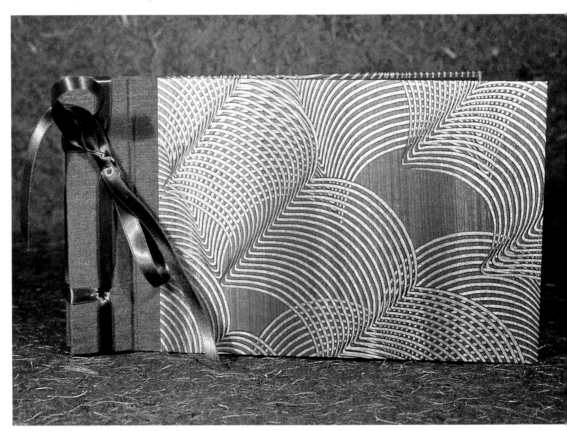

The hardcover photo album or scrapbook.

A

wider than the hinge board. Then cut two pieces of book cloth to line the hinge. The liners should be about 1 inch (2.5 cm) wider and ¼ inch (0.6 cm) shorter than the hinge board measurement.

CREATING THE HINGED COVER

Apply glue to one of the hinge boards and place it on the larger piece of book cloth so that a ³/₄-inch (1-cm) margin extends from the top, bottom, and left-hand edges of the board. Turn over the glued hinge and attached book cloth and burnish it to smooth out the glued area. Turn it wrong-side up again, over a piece of scrap paper. Cut the corners of the cloth (to the left of the hinge) on a diagonal to miter them. Then place a ¹/₈-inch-wide (0.3-cm-wide) balsa or Plexiglas spacer next to the spine. (Or measure and place the boards about ¹/₈ inch [0.3 cm] apart.) Apply glue to all edges of the book cloth, being sure to also apply glue to the lip of the cover boards as you run your brush along them. Place one of the cover boards next to the ¹/₈-inch (0.3-cm) spacer, lining up the top and bottom edges of the cover board with those of the hinge board (see **step A**). Remove the ¹/₈-inch (0.3-cm) spacer and brush a bit of glue in the gap.

B

Turn the boards book-cloth-side up, and, using the bone folder, smooth the book cloth into the hinge groove and onto the cover board. Flip the book board over again (see **step B**), and then, starting at the head and tail (top and bottom) of the cover, fold over and burnish the book-cloth flaps in place. Make a neat mitered corner with a bone folder (see **step C**) before turning the book cloth over at the spine of the book. Be sure to burnish the hinge groove on the inside of the book, too (see **step D**).

C

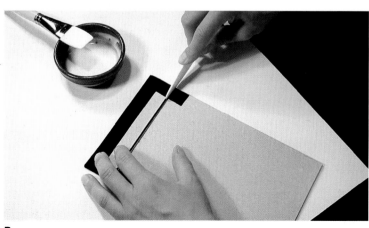

D

APPLYING THE HINGE LINER

Brush glue on the smaller piece of book cloth and press it into place, just inside the left edge of the hinge board you just covered (see **step E**). Part of the book cloth will extend onto the inside of the cover board. Lightly position it and then bend the hinge of the book away from you to mimic the action of opening the cover. This will move the glued cloth slightly to the left, assuring that the hinge has the give necessary to the proper functioning of the book. When the liner is properly positioned, burnish it down, running the bone folder into the hinge grooves as you work.

E

F

APPLYING THE COVER PAPERS

Now it's time to cover the boards with your paste papers. Paste papers for wrapping the cover boards should have a vertical grain direction and be 1¹/₂ inches (4 cm) taller — but need to be only ¹/₂ inch (1 cm) wider — than the cover boards to allow for a ³/₄-inch (2-cm) turnover on three sides. (Because the book cloth extends onto the cover board, and the paste paper need not cover all of it, the cover paper will begin about ¹/₄ inch [0.6 cm] in from the left edge of the board.)

Measure about ¹/₄ inch (0.6 cm) away from the hinge groove (away from the spine and toward the fore edge of the book), and pencil a faint positioning line on the book cloth. Working over scrap paper, brush glue on the front of the cover board and very lightly on the narrow section of book cloth to the right of the line you just penciled in. Apply the cover paper to the pasted board (see **step F**), overlapping the pencil line slightly and making sure that the paper extends at least ³/₄ inch (2 cm) on the top, bottom, and fore edge (right-hand side) of the cover. Burnish the paper in place. Flip the cover over, miter the corners as you did in the first project, apply glue to the top and bottom paper flaps, fold them over, and burnish them down (see **step G**). Then glue, fold over, and burnish the side flaps in place, making neat folded corners.

G

LINING THE COVER

Cut a piece of text-weight paper $1/2$ inch (1 cm) smaller than the cover board (not the entire cover), and, working from the center outward, spread glue on it. Center one end of it, glue-side down, $1/4$ inch (0.6 cm) in from the left edge of the cover board. Use the bone folder to smooth it down toward the right edge. Burnish it in place. Encase the finished book cover in waxed paper. So that it dries flat, press it overnight or until dry.

Repeat the preceding steps to cover the second book cover or, if you prefer, make the back cover in one piece without the hinge.

MAKING THE INTERIOR PAGES

Cut or tear 20 to 24 cover-weight pages to use as the interior of the book. These should be $1/2$ inch (1 cm) smaller than the height of the book and $1/4$ inch (0.6 cm) smaller than the length of it. (This allows for a $1/4$-inch [0.6-cm] margin on three sides when the pages are aligned with the spine edge.) To thicken the spine edge of the book block (the stack of pages) and allow the book to lay flat when photos are incorporated, spacers or fillers should be added between the pages. These can be made from the same material as the book pages. They should be as wide as the hinge board and the same height as the pages. Using a glue stick to tack them in place on the spine edge of each page will keep them in position during drilling or hole punching.

PREPARING TO DRILL OR PUNCH HOLES

Make a paper template the same size as the hinge board for marking where the cover and page holes should be made. Draw a line down the center of the paper and make two marks on this line, an equal

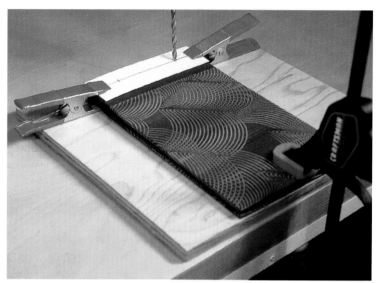

H

distance in from the top and bottom edges of the paper. Mine are $1 1/4$ inches (3 cm) in from the edges.

Gather and align the album pages and spacers and center them, flush with the spine, between the book covers before clamping them together with the template on the top of the stack (see **step H**).

CREATING STITCHING HOLES

Work over several pieces of either scrap book board or a conventional board and use a clamp to stabilize the book by attaching it to a table, if drilling holes. Choose a $1/4$-inch (0.6-cm) bit for your electric or hand drill to accommodate a ribbon binding like that shown on page 88. If punching holes, use the template to mark where holes should be made in the covers. After punching cover holes, center one page spacer below the cover to mark where the page holes should be punched. Use that spacer as a page hole template, clamping it over stacks of pages and spacers or fillers to mark the exact position for repeated punching with a screw punch or rubber mallet and punch set.

CREATING THE EDGE-SEWN BINDING

The stitching material for this two-hole album will pass through each of the spine holes three times. Keeping this in mind, choose a ribbon, braid, or strong nonstretching cord that coordinates with the 1/4-inch (0.6-cm) hole you made. The length of your stitching material should be about seven times the height of your book cover. After drilling or punching sewing holes, keep your book clamped to keep the cover and page holes lined up. Then begin stitching as follows:

1. Enter the top hole in the front cover, leaving a tail of ribbon about 9 inches (23 cm) long. This length will allow you to tie your ribbon in a bow, as pictured.
2. Wrap the ribbon over the head of the book, and sew back into the same hole. (Pull the ribbon taut as you continue stitching.)
3. Sew around the spine of the book and into the hole a third time, exiting on the back cover.
4. Sew across the back of the book and bring the ribbon up into the second hole at the tail end of the book.
5. Sew around the spine of the book and up into this hole a second time.
6. Wrap the ribbon over the tail edge of the book and sew up into the hole a third time, exiting on the album front.
7. Tie the ends of the ribbon together in a bow to finish.

If you are stitching with bookbinders' thread or embroidery floss and intend to end with a knot instead of a decorative bow, you won't need to allow for such a long piece of stitching material. Should you clip close to the ends of a knotted stitching material, however, it's a good idea to put a tiny spot of glue on the knot to hold it securely. Another option is to poke the ends of thread and the knot into a sewing hole to hide them.

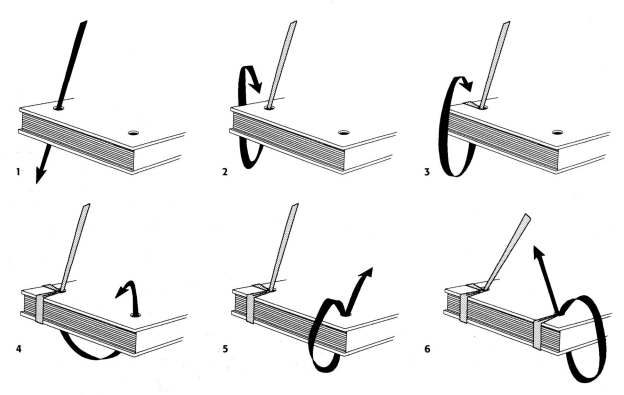

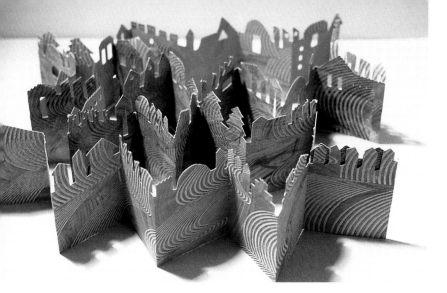

Depending on the techniques used, paste papers can add drama or whimsy to a project. The book artists whose works are shown here have used paste papers to create remarkable flag and accordion-fold books.

TOP: Folding City, *an accordion-fold book by Jan Owen. 5 × 144 in. (13 × 366 cm) open.*

CENTER: Ocean Blooms, *an artist's book by Mary Howe. 5¹/₂ × 6 × 1¹/₄ in. (14 × 15 × 3 cm). Photo by Ken Woisard.*

BOTTOM: Chameleons on Parade *by Anne-Claude Cotty. This artist's book, with vibrant paste-paper designs that reveal underpaintings, is 10 × 12 × 1 in. (25 × 30 × 2.5 cm) closed; 28 in. (71 cm) open. Photo by Darwin Davidson.*

Picture Mat

MATERIALS

- Precut mat or extra mat board
- Mat board
- Pencil
- Metal-edged ruler
- Utility knife
- Cutting mat
- Lightweight to medium-weight paste paper
- Glue or dry adhesive
- Large and small glue brushes
- Burnisher
- Book cloth (optional)
- Awl
- $1/4$-inch-wide (0.6-cm-wide) ribbon
- Photo to place in the finished mat
- Acetate to place over photo (optional)

This freestanding picture mat can be made in any size to frame and display your favorite photo. Start with a purchased mat, or cut your own from a piece of mat board. It's fun to make an assortment of mats that coordinate with each other to form a grouping of photos for a library table or desk. You can create patterned paste papers in grays and blacks with metallic paints over them that will coordinate with most photos, or create mats to go with favorite photos, choosing paste-paper colors to complement the scenery or clothing the subject in the photo is wearing.

CUTTING YOUR OWN MAT

To make a mat for a 5- × 7-inch (13- × 18-cm) photo, cut out an 8- × 10-inch (20- × 25-cm) piece of mat board while working over the cutting mat. Using a pencil and ruler, place rule lines $1^3/4$ inches (4 cm) in from the top and bottom edges of the board and $1^3/4$ inches (4 cm) in from either side of the board. With a metal-edged rule and a utility knife, cut out the $4^1/2$- × $6^1/2$-inch (11- × 17-cm) window formed by the intersecting lines. Be sure that cuts are parallel, but don't worry about overcuts—they won't show. You should now have a mat with $1^3/4$-inch (4-cm) borders all around.

COVERING THE MAT

Cut a piece of paste paper so that it is one inch (2.5 cm) larger all around than the mat you've created. Apply glue or dry adhesive to the front of the mat, and center it on the back of the paste paper. (If your paste paper has horizontal or vertical designs that must line up with your mat edges, draw positioning guidelines so that you can accurately center the mat.) Turn the mat over, burnish the paper down, and then flip it over again to

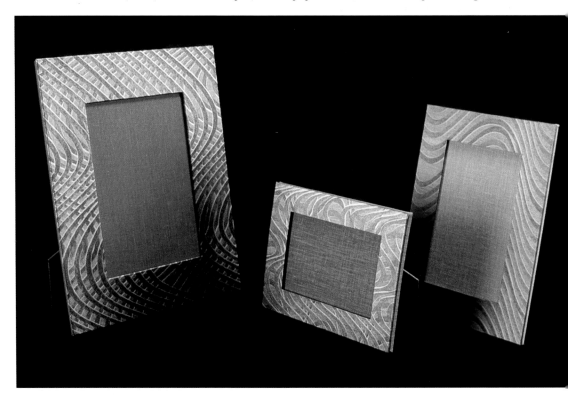

Simple yet sophisticated paste-paper designs in metallic colors decorate these freestanding mats by Myrna Bendett.

expose the uncovered mat. Use your utility knife to cut diagonal slits (an "x") in the windowed area, ending each line just a bit away from the corner of the window. Cut out the center of the window to create narrow paper flaps. Then apply glue and fold the window flaps over onto the inside of the mat, as shown in **step A**. Burnish the flaps down.

Apply glue and fold the paper around the outside edges of the mat, too, following the directions previously given (see page 83) for mitering corners. Burnish the glued areas and, if you used a liquid glue, press the mat until dry.

CREATING THE MAT BACKING

To make the backing for the mat, cut another 8- × 10-inch (20- × 25-cm) piece of mat board and cover it with paste paper, too, burnishing the paper to smooth it down. Then cut another slightly smaller piece of paste paper or coordinating piece of book cloth to cover the edges of the paper you just burnished down. Your backing is now completely encased in paste paper. Although part of the backing (the smaller piece of paper or book cloth you just glued down) will not show when a photo is inserted in your mat, the extra step will make the mat more presentable if given as a gift unadorned with a photo. Press the backing until dry.

CREATING A CHANNEL FOR THE PHOTO

To create a channel to keep the photo from slipping within the mat, cut three mat board strips each $^1/_2$ inch (1.3 cm) wide. The two for the window sides should be about $7^1/_2$ inches (19 cm) long, and the one for the bottom about 6 inches (15 cm) long. Glue these to the bottom and side edges of the back of the windowed mat, leaving about a $^3/_8$-inch (1 cm) space between them and the edge of the window, as shown in **step B**.

A

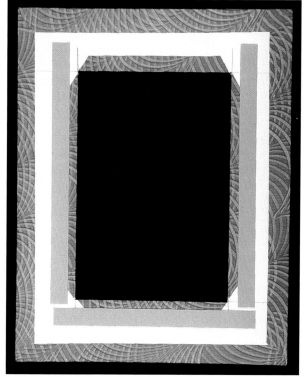

B

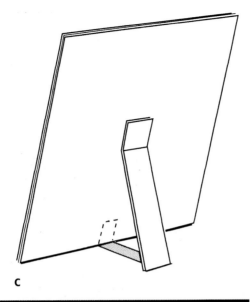

C

D

CREATING THE MAT STAND

To create a mat-board support so your picture mat will be freestanding, cut a piece of board measuring 1¹/₂ inches (4 cm) wide by 7 inches (18 cm) long. Score it about an inch down from the top so it can be bent, as shown in **step C**, to support the mat. Cover the front of the stand with paste paper. Cut a 4-inch (10-cm) piece of coordinating ¹/₄-inch (0.6-cm) ribbon, and glue a 1-inch (2.5-cm) end of it onto the bottom back of the stand. Then line the back of the stand with another strip of paste paper to hide the ribbon's end.

Position the mat stand in the center of the mat back by lining up the bottom of the stand with the bottom of the mat back. Mark the position and then glue the 1-inch (2.5-cm) scored section of the stand to the back of the mat. Wrap 1 inch (2.5-cm) of the ribbon under the mat and glue it inside the mat back, as shown in **step C**. This ribbon will keep the picture mat standing correctly.

ASSEMBLING THE MAT

To assemble the picture mat, glue the mat board strips to the mat back, forming the channel for the picture. The top of the picture mat is left open (see **step D**) so a photo and protective sheet of clear acetate (from an art-supply store) can be slipped in, if desired.

TIP

Book cloth could be used to cover the back of the mat and wrap the mat stand, or you could make a mat back and stand out of solid-core black mat board or suede-covered mat board and omit the covering steps entirely. Picture-frame suppliers, like United Manufacturers Supplies, also sell mat backs with attached easel stands that can be used to support the standing mats you create.

A VARIATION: THE FRAMED MIRROR

You can easily create a small, paste-paper framed mirror to grace a side table by following some of the instructions for cutting and covering a mat listed in the previous project. Cut your mat as suggested or start with a purchased one. Instead of using a piece of paste paper 1 inch (2.5 cm) larger all around than your mat, however, start with a paste paper 2 inches (5 cm) larger all around. Glue your mat in the center of this paper, and cut out and cover the window area. Burnish everything down, and, if using a liquid adhesive, press the mat until the glue is dry.

Have a thin piece of mirror cut to the same size as your mat, and, using a strong glue designed for paper and glass, glue the mirror to the back of the mat board so that edges are flush. Glue a piece of mat board over the back of the mirror. Miter the corners of your paste paper and wrap them around the sandwich of mat board and mirror, gluing and burnishing them flat. To finish, glue a large piece of paste paper over the exposed edges of paper.

The mirror shown here was made to rest in a decorative stand. A stand like the one created in the previous project will function fine if you make it wide enough to support the weight of the mirror. Or you can attach an appropriate hanger to the back of the mirror to mount it on the wall.

A paste-paper framed mirror.

Covered Lamp Shade

A paste-paper-covered lamp shade is easy to make. Although the paste paper will not allow much light to shine through the shade, the soft glow around the decorated shade will add a bit of drama to a dark corner of a room. The shade pictured was made by Grace Taormina of Rubber Stampede. Grace coated a heavy piece of watercolor paper with paste and then stamped it with a foam leaf stamp to remove some of the color. Next she coated a foam stamp with dark green paste and stamped it over the previous design.

An existing lamp shade was rolled and its path was marked on heavy paper to create a pattern with the shade's dimensions. Using the pattern, the paste paper was cut to size and glued on top of an existing white shade. An even easier method of covering a shade is to purchase a self-adhesive lamp shade. Such shades have a liner that you peel off and use as a pattern. When you've cut your paste paper to the correct size, you just place it on the adhesive-covered shade. Fabric or paper trim can then be added to cover the top and bottom edges of the shade.

A lamp shade covered in paste papers by Grace Taormina. Stamps provided by Rubber Stampede.

Another way to create a shade cover (preferably for a small lamp) is to accordion-pleat a long sheet of paste paper (or glue several pleated sheets together). If you then punch ribbon holes ½ inch (1.3 cm) down from the top of each pleat and overlap and glue the ends of the sheet together, you can gather the shade with a length of ribbon, adjust the pleats, and slip it over an existing white shade. A long line ruled across the top of the paper, ½ inch (1.3 cm) down from the top, will help you keep your ribbon holes even.

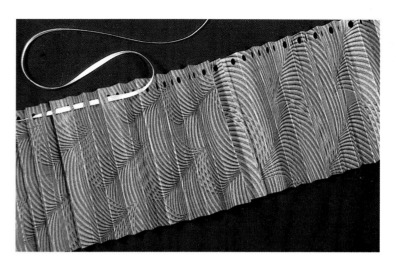

ABOVE: *Gathering the accordion folds of the pleated lamp shade.*

LEFT: *An accordion-folded lamp shade for a small boudoir lamp.*

Woven Basket

MATERIALS

- 140-pound watercolor paper measuring 20 × 30 inches (51 × 76 cm), paste-painted on both sides
- Pasta cutter (or metal-edged yardstick and X-Acto knife)
- Scissors
- Pencil
- Pushpins
- Felt
- Wood, florist's foam, or foam house insulation (for weaving mold)
- Small clips
- #18 tapestry needle
- 4 yards waxed linen or other thick thread
- White glue
- Acrylic spray varnish

Paste-paper weaving strips:

- *Rims:* 2, each 30 inches (76 cm) long by $\frac{1}{2}$ inch (1.3 cm) wide
- *Uprights or warp strips:* 26, each 12 inches (30 cm) long by $\frac{1}{4}$ inch (0.6 cm) wide (or fettuccini setting on pasta cutter)
- *Weavers or weft strips:* 9, each 30 inches (76 cm) long by $\frac{1}{4}$ inch (0.6 cm) wide (or fettuccini setting on pasta cutter)

This festive paste-paper basket with its wonderful relief curls is a project contributed by Patti Quinn Hill. She suggests using the basket to hold napkins, but Mardi Gras beads, notepaper, tiny pine cones, or even dried flower petals would also look great displayed in such a container. The three-dimensional weaving on this basket follows the simple over/under tabby-weave design we learned in grade school. Once you learn the basics of three-dimensional paste-paper weaving, lots of variations can be made to create larger or smaller works or baskets in various shapes. The project is not difficult, but cutting the weaving strips can be time consuming. Patti has found a great way to cut them using a pasta cutter, making any paste-paper project calling for thin strips of paper much easier. A good-quality paper shredder that does not cut strips with serrated edges will also do the job.

CREATING THE MOLD

A wooden or dense foam block should be made to support the weaving as you work. The ideal mold for this basket would be made of two pieces of wood, glued together to form a block. Although a square block could be used, making a mold with tapered sides, as shown below, is recommended. If your finished weaving is tight, it may be difficult to remove from a nonsloping mold.

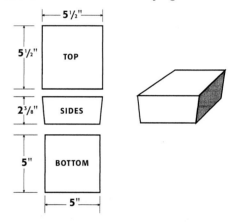

A paste-paper woven basket by Patti Quinn Hill. $5\frac{1}{2} \times 5\frac{1}{2} \times 2\frac{1}{2}$ in. (14 × 14 × 6 cm).

A

CREATING THE WEAVING STRIPS

Cut two ¹⁄₂-inch-wide (1.3-cm-wide) pieces 30 inches (76 cm) long for the rims.

For the uprights, insert 4 inches (10 cm) of paper (paper's full length equals 30 inches [76 cm]) through a pasta cutter. (This will yield some excess paper scraps, which you can use in other projects.) From this cut 26 pieces, each 12 inches (30 cm) long.

For the weavers, insert 3 inches (8 cm) of paper through the pasta cutter. Leave the weavers at their full length (30 inches [76 cm]).

LAYING OUT THE BASE

1. Take 2 uprights and put a light pencil mark in the center of each one. Cross these two pieces at the mark. These will be your center uprights. Keep track of your center.

2. Weave 2 uprights on all sides of these center pieces for a total of 10 uprights, 5 going in each direction (see **step A**). Have the negative spaces between the uprights be about ¹⁄₈ inch (0.3 cm), and make sure that the ends of the uprights line up.

3. Add 4 more uprights on each side horizontally, making sure ends are lined up. After all 13 uprights are woven in horizontally and 5 are woven in vertically, place the base on the bottom of the mold to see if the 13 uprights fit. Do any necessary adjusting on the 13 uprights at this time. (It is easier to adjust these 13 when there are only 5 going vertically.) Secure this preliminary base with clips (see **step B**).

4. Add 4 uprights on each side of the center. Place the basket base on the bottom of the mold and make adjustments so that the base fits exactly all the way around. There should be 13 uprights woven in each direction.

5. Decide which side will be the outside of your basket. Place the outside of the basket face up, and upsett all of the uprights. (The term "upsett" means to put a sharp

B

C

crease by folding the uprights along the edges of the woven base.)

6. Secure the woven base onto the mold using pushpins. Place tiny pieces of felt between the basket and the pushpins so that the pushpins do not mark the basket (see **step C**).

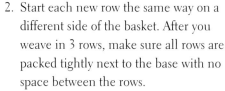

WEAVING UP THE SIDES

1. Make sure your first row of weaving is opposite the base weaving, going over one under one. Start the weaver (the weft) on an upright (the warp), clipping it in position as shown (see **step D**). Weave snugly all the way around the mold; when you get back to where you started, stabilize the row by continuing to weave through 4 uprights, ending by hiding the weaver under an upright. Cut the weaver flush with the edge of that upright so that it is hidden. Never do overlaps around a corner.

2. Start each new row the same way on a different side of the basket. After you weave in 3 rows, make sure all rows are packed tightly next to the base with no space between the rows.

3. Always start each new row by clipping the weaver in place over an upright and ending it by weaving it through an additional 4 uprights and stopping under one. Weave to the top of the mold doing 7 rows. Keep each row packed tightly to the row below, with no space between the rows. Make sure the uprights continue to stay evenly spaced.

CREATING THE CURLS

1. Place a row of curls on top of row 7, completely covering it. Start your curl by weaving under an upright, attaching a clip to secure the weaver. Wrap the piece completely around, making a small circle, and then place the weaver under the next upright and so on, making curls all the way around the row. The curls should sit on top of every other upright, as shown in **step E,** and are secured each time the weaver passes under the next upright. Continue around the basket in this way, making all the curls uniform in size.

2. You may need to splice a piece in to complete the row of curls. If so, splice under an upright, overlapping the pieces, thus making a double thickness. Clip the splice to hold it securely until you get the next row of weaving in above it.

3. When you get to the end of the row of curls, cut and hide the end of the weaver behind the upright where you started. This will make a double thickness here.

4. Weave row 8, and then add another row of curls covering it. Weave in row 9 with no curls.

D

E

REMOVING THE WEAVING

1. Twist the pushpins, removing them from the mold, and then pull the basket off the mold.

2. Cut all uprights on the outside of the basket so that they are flush with the top of the last row of weaving. Fold all uprights on the inside of the basket over to the outside, and cut them just above the bottom of the last row of weaving. Using white glue, glue these folded strips down to the last row of weaving and clip to dry (see **step F**). After the glue dries, remove the clips.

ATTACHING THE INSIDE RIM

Take one of the ¹/₂-inch-wide (1.3-cm-wide) strips of paper and cut off the corners, giving the strip a point. Place this point on the inside of the basket at one of the right corners, and clip it on the basket, making sure that it does not go below the last row of weaving. Clip the strip snugly all the way around the basket (see **step G**). When you return to where you started, overlap this piece halfway around that side (about 3 inches [8 cm] into the side). Create a point on the end of this piece, too.

CREATING THE OUTSIDE RIM

Start clipping the outside rim on the same side of the basket where you started the inside rim. Place it halfway over where your inside overlap ended. Clip snugly all the way around so that it's flush with the bottom of the last row of weaving.

When you get back to where you started, overlap to the corner of that side and cut the end of the strip into a point. Both of the overlaps should be on the same side of the basket. This will give you room for adjustment at the end of the lashing.

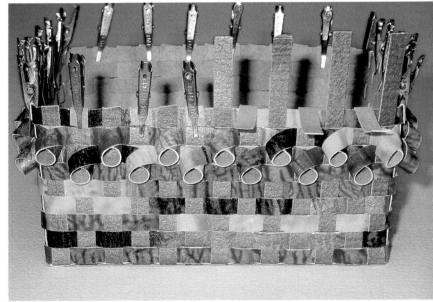

F

G

LASHING

1. Thread the needle with the lashing thread, and, working from the outside of the basket, insert the needle going upward in the narrow space between the inside of the basket and the inside rim. Start

between the third and fourth uprights to the right of the outside rim overlap. Pull the thread up and over the top of the basket, leaving a 4-inch (10-cm) tail of thread hanging down on the outside of the basket. Insert the needle in the narrow space between the outside of the basket

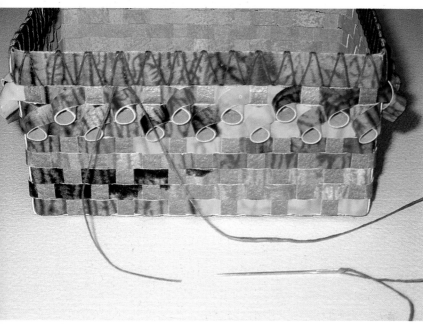

H

and the outside rim and bring the lashing inside the basket again.

Now lash around the rims by bringing the needle over to the outside of the basket and inserting it into the basket between each upright, lashing around and around the rim. Always insert the needle and thread from the outside and pull the thread from the inside (see **step H**). Pull tightly all around the basket, making sure not to lose tension.

2. When you get to where you started your lashing and all spaces between the uprights have been filled, turn back and go the other way, making Vs on the rim with the thread. This is called double lashing. Go all the way around and through each space until you reach the point where the lashing was originally started.

3. After you have put the needle in the last space and pulled the thread inside the basket and there are Vs above every upright, it is time to tie it off (see **step I**). Place the needle going upward between the inside rim and the inside of the basket, up and over the top of the basket, and then insert the needle downward between the outside rim and the outside of the basket, pulling snugly. Tie a square knot, hiding it under the rim, and cut the tails.

FINISHING

Spray the basket with an acrylic varnish to stiffen it.

Practice your basket-weaving skills on other forms to make paste-paper baskets in a variety of shapes and sizes. Be sure to explore other weaving designs by tearing or cutting the vertical warp strips or horizontal weft strips into a variety of different widths with smooth, serrated, or deckled edges.

I

LEFT: Copper Urn, *a woven basket by Patti Quinn Hill. A wooden mold was used to begin this basket, but other objects, such as a balloon (later popped), could instead be used to give form to a basket. 11 × 9 in. (28 × 23 cm).*

BELOW: Peacocks. *Paste-paper woven baskets by Patti Quinn Hill. Various types of molds can be used to create woven baskets. Although Patti employed a wooden structure known as a "shaker mold" to begin Peacocks, glass bottles could also be used, remaining as part of the work. 15 × 6 in. (38 × 15 cm), 17 × 8 in. (43 × 20 cm), 12 × 7 in. (30 × 18 cm).*

Paste-Paper Box

MATERIALS

- Book board or heavy mat board
- Pencil
- Cutting tools: a utility knife and a metal square or a professional paper or board cutter
- PVA glue
- Large and small glue brushes
- Masking tape (optional)
- Lightweight to medium-weight paste paper
- Awl
- Methylcellulose adhesive
- Scrap paper
- Tracing paper (optional)
- Bone folder
- Box support (optional)
- Scissors
- Book cloth (optional)

A small paste-paper box or, even better, a collection of paste-paper boxes of various sizes will offer a delightful accent in any room. Although they will be convenient places to stash paper clips, rubber bands, or other flotsam and jetsam in an office or living room, you may not want to use these in such a utilitarian fashion. They are so inviting that guests will no doubt be driven to lift their lids. A single feather or a tiny shell will be a more fitting occupant for these charming containers. Kelsey Woodward contributed both the partially completed and finished box shown in the accompanying photos.

The directions, most of which Kelsey provided, are adapted from *Books, Boxes and Wraps* by Marilyn Webberley and JoAn Forsyth. This and other books focusing on box making are listed on page 110. All have excellent tips for making a version of the box shown here.

BEGINNING THE BOX

Determine the size of your box—its width, length, and height—and the board grain. (For this project, the grain of the book board and of the paste-paper covering should run parallel to the box wall length.)

Using the cutting tool you have chosen:

- Cut the base to reflect the length and width dimensions of the box.
- Cut 2 sides to the width of the box by the height of the box.
- Cut 2 sides to equal the length of the box plus two board thicknesses, by the height of the box.
- Cut the lid: the box base width plus 4 board thicknesses, by the box base length plus 4 board thicknesses.
- Cut the lid liner: the box base width minus 1 board thickness, by the box base length minus one board thickness plus a tiny bit.

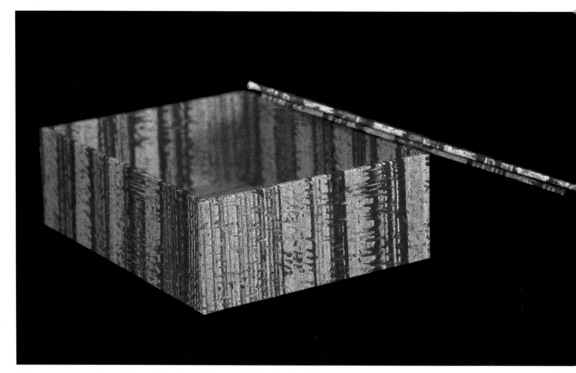

The paste-paper box Kelsey Woodward designed for this book. Buttons or paper beads could be added to decorate the lid. $3^1/_2 \times 4^1/_2 \times 1^3/_8$ in. (9 × 11 × 3 cm).

Assemble the box by brushing PVA glue along the wall edges where they meet the base board and each other. Glue up one board at a time, using masking tape to hold outside corners together until adhesive sets, if necessary.

COVERING THE BOX

This method uses one continuous piece of paste paper to cover the outside and inside walls of the box.

The length of the paper should be twice the length of wall A, plus twice the length of wall B, plus 4 board thicknesses, plus $^1/_2$ inch (1.3 cm). The width of the paper should be twice the height of a box wall, plus 1 board thickness, plus 1 inch (2.5 cm).

On the wrong side of this paper, use an awl to score a $^1/_2$-inch (1.3-cm) margin down the left side and along the bottom edge. Gently fold along the score lines. Follow the directions below to brush adhesive (a mixture of three-quarters PVA glue and one-quarter methylcellulose) on the box boards rather than on the paste paper.

Brush the adhesive mixture on the outside of one side wall of the box. Set it in place along the scored lines of the paste paper. Press the paste paper against the box wall (see **step A**).

Place a clean piece of tracing or scrap paper over the paste paper and smooth the paste paper down with a bone folder. Work in the direction of the grain to avoid stretching the paste paper.

Continue this process one wall at a time. To avoid air bubbles, work the paste paper around each corner by pulling it with one hand and pressing it to the box wall with the other.

For the last wall, brush adhesive on the entire wall and press down the $^1/_2$-inch (1.3-cm) flap. Brush adhesive lightly onto

A completed box bottom, shown with the book-board parts used to create the box bottom and the two-part lid.

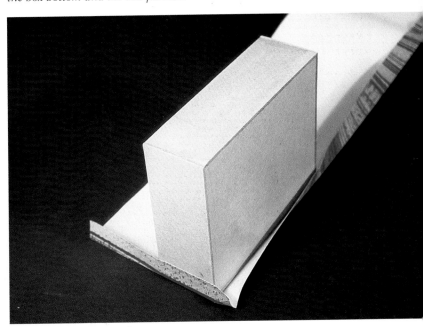

A

the edge of the paste paper that overlaps this flap. Pull the paste paper around the corner and smooth the last wall covering into place.

Be sure to frequently rotate the box as you smooth down the wall covering with your bone folder.

B

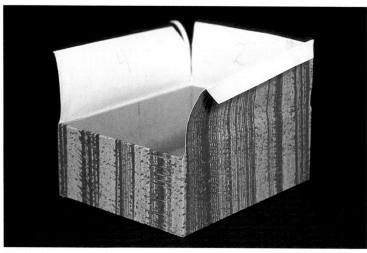

C

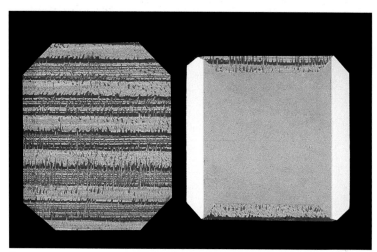

D

To miter the outside corners of the box base, hold the box upside down, or prop it up by placing it over a support. Pinch together the excess paper. Hold your scissors parallel to the box bottom. Keep enough paste paper at the corner point to cover the base board and then clip off the excess (see **step B**). Adhere edges in place with adhesive.

PREPARING TO LINE THE INSIDE

The following easy method of cutting a slit in the paper used to line the box walls will work with small boxes. Larger boxes may require the use of a triangle to determine the size of the triangular-shaped slit.

Turn the box right-side up, and at each corner cut a *very* narrow triangular-shaped slit down to the top of the box. This cutaway slit should not be wider than the board thickness. If it is, part of the wall will remain uncovered and will show when the box is lined.

Fold one short wall into the box and crease it along the bottom of the box. Unfold, measure the width of the crease, and score this measurement on the other folds. Remove a 45-degree corner from the edges of each end of the creased flaps (see **step C**).

PASTING DOWN THE LINING WALLS

Begin pasting the short walls first, one wall at a time. Brush adhesive on the top edge of the box, the inside wall, and the narrow adjoining area of the box base where the lining will overlap.

Pull the lining over the top edge of the box and press and rub with a bone folder. Pull the lining to the inside of the box and press it onto the inside walls. Smooth it into place with a bone folder. Repeat.

COVERING THE BASE

Apply to the inside and outside of the box base a covering material made from additional paste paper or book cloth that is slightly smaller than the box base, about ¹/₈ inch (0.3 cm) all around.

Spread adhesive on the linings and set them in place. Press them down with your fingers and then smooth with a bone folder.

CREATING THE LID

The lid consists of two parts, with the smaller covered board (the lid liner) resting inside the box to keep the lid in place. Cover both parts with paste paper (see **step D**), following the directions for covering the accordion-fold book boards on page 83. Then glue them together, with the wrong side of the smaller paper-covered board centered on the wrong side of the larger one. Note: If you wish to stitch buttons, beads, or a tassel to adorn the box lid, do so before the smaller lid liner is glued in place so the stitching material is hidden between the boards. An awl can be used to create a stitching hole.

Practice your box-making skills on a few small rectangular models before moving on to other shapes with or without lids. There are a number of books solely devoted to box making that can help you create other designs, like the triangular box shown on page 6.

Look for courses in book and box making, often offered through universities and art centers, to expand your knowledge. If you practice your paste-painting and paper-art skills, you'll soon develop your own unique style of paste-paper design and use it to advantage on artwork like that shown throughout this book. Many of the works shown were chosen because they were created by artists who not only produce their own paste papers but also create artworks with them. It is hoped that you will find inspiration here to encourage you to continue both your paste-paper and your paper-art adventures.

Lidded box by Kelsey Woodward. By using complex paste papers with many layers of color and adding button and bead ornamentation, Kelsey has transformed this box from a utilitarian object into a piece of art. Photo by John Sheldon.

Further Reading

Hollander, Annette. *Easy to Make Decorative Boxes and Desk Accessories.* New York: Dover, 1986.

Johnson, Pauline. *Creative Bookbinding.* Seattle: University of Washington Press, 1963.

LaPlantz, Shereen. *Cover to Cover.* Asheville, N.C.: Lark Books, 1995.

Loring, Rosamond B. *Decorated Book Papers.* Cambridge, Mass.: Harvard College Library, 1973.

Maurer-Mathison, Diane, with Jennifer Philippoff. *Paper Art.* New York: Watson-Guptill Publications, 1997.

Maurer-Mathison, Diane. *Art of the Scrapbook.* New York: Watson-Guptill Publications, 2000.

Mauriello, Barbara. *Making Memory Boxes.* Gloucester, Mass.: Rockport Publishers, 2000.

Maziarczyk, Claire. *Miniature Pastepapers.* Marcham, England: The Alembic Press, 1998.

Smith, Keith A., and Fred A. Jordan. *Bookbinding for Book Artists.* New York: Keith Smith Books, 1998.

Webberley, Marilyn, and JoAn Forsyth. *Books, Boxes and Wraps.* Kirkland, Wash.: Bifocal Publishing, 1995.

Zeier, Franz. *Books, Boxes, and Portfolios.* New York: Design Press, 1990.

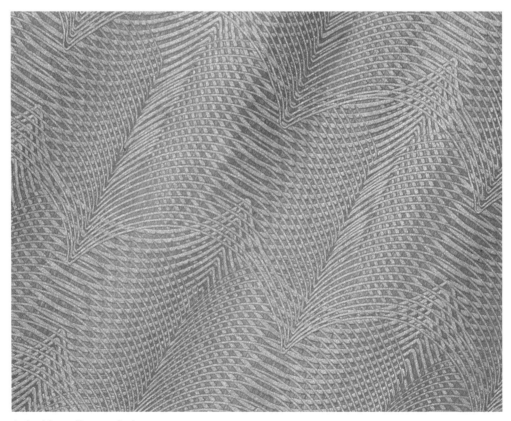

A double scallop combed paste paper.

Source Directory

Amsterdam Art
1013 University Avenue
Berkeley, CA 94710
(510) 649-4800
www.amsterdamart.com
Art supplies, paper

Bookmakers
6001 66th Avenue
Suite 101
Riverdale, MD 20737
(301) 927-7787
www.bookmakerscatalog.com
Binding supplies

Colophon Book Arts Supply
3611 Ryan Street S.E.
Lacey, WA 98503
(360) 459-2940
Binding supplies

Colwood Electronics
15 Meridian Road
Eatontown, NJ 07724
(732) 544-1119
www.woodburning.com
Wood-burning tools

Daniel Smith
P.O. Box 84268
Seattle, WA 98124-5568
(800) 426-6740
www.danielsmith.com
Art supplies, papers

Diane Maurer
P.O. Box 78
Spring Mills, PA 16875
(814) 422-8651
www.dianemaurer.com
Paste-paper combs, decorative papers, marbling supplies

Factory Express
1720 Coulter
Rio Rancho, NM 87124
(800) 399-2564
www.factory-express.com
Kutrimmer paper and board cutter

Fascinating Folds
P.O. Box 10070
Glendale, AZ 85318
(480) 471-1123
www.fascinating-folds.com
Papers, books, paper art supplies

Flax Art and Design
1699 Market Street
San Francisco, CA 94103
(415) 552-2355
www.flaxart.com
Papers, art supplies

Hollanders
407 North Fifth Avenue
Ann Arbor, MI 48104
(734) 741-7531
www.hollanders.com
Decorative papers, bookbinding supplies

John Neal, Bookseller
1833 Spring Garden Street
Greensboro, NC 27403
(800) 369-9598
www.johnnealbooks.com
Books, calligraphy supplies

Light Impressions
439 Monroe Avenue
Rochester, NY 14603-0940
(800) 828-6216
www.lightimpressionsdirect.com
Archival art supplies

Mainely Shades
100 Gray Road
Falmouth, ME 04105
(800) 554-1755
www.mainelyshades.com
Lamp shade materials

Paper & Ink Books
3 North Second Street
Woodsboro, MD 21798
(301) 898-7991
www.paperinkbooks.com
Books, calligraphy supplies

Paper Source, Inc.
232 West Chicago
Chicago, IL 60610
(312) 337-0798
Large selection of papers

Pearl Paint Co. Inc.
308 Canal Street
New York, NY 10013-2572
(800) 451-PEARL
www.pearlpaint.com
Art supplies, paper

Ranger
15 Park Road
Tinton Falls, NJ 07724
(732) 389-3535
www.rangerink.com
Inks, brayers, art stamp accessories

University Products, Inc.
517 Main Street
Holyoke, MA 01041-0101
(800) 628-1912
www.archivalsuppliers.com
Archival bookmaking supplies

Index